SPECIAL *flip*

C0-APH-099

Women on Men

{ Love and Life with the Opposite Sex }

EDITED BY BARB KARG

ADAMS MEDIA
AVON, MASSACHUSETTS

Published by
Adams Media, an F+W Publications Company
57 Littlefield Street
Avon, MA 02322. U.S.A.
www.adamsmedia.com

ISBN 10: 1-59337-732-0
ISBN 13: 978-1-59337-732-8

Printed in Canada.

J I H G F E D C B A

Library of Congress Cataloging-in-Publication Data
is available from the publisher.

This publication is designed to provide accurate and authoritative information with regard to the subject matter covered. It is sold with the understanding that the publisher is not engaged in rendering legal, accounting, or other professional advice. If legal advice or other expert assistance is required, the services of a competent professional person should be sought.

> —From a *Declaration of Principles* jointly adopted by a
> Committee of the American Bar Association and
> a Committee of Publishers and Associations

Many of the designations used by manufacturers and sellers to distinguish their product are claimed as trademarks. Where those designations appear in this book and Adams Media was aware of a trademark claim, the designations have been printed with initial capital letters.

This book is available at quantity discounts for bulk purchases.
For information, please call 1-800-289-0963.

FOR SISSY

May your life be filled with love, peace, joy, and comfort. And if all else fails—try chocolate.

AND FOR RICK

My life, my love.

ACKNOWLEDGMENTS

Many fine individuals took part in the making of this book. As always, I'd like to thank Rick, Ma, Pop, Chris, Glen, Dad, Anne, Terry, Kathy, the Blonde Bombshell, Ellen, Jeans, all the Jims, Karla, and the Scribe Tribe. I adore you all.

I'd also like to extend a big thank you to the fine folks at Adams Media for all their hard work, including acquisitions editor extraordinaire Paula Munier, assistant editor Andrea Norville, associate production editor Casey Ebert, and senior book designer Colleen Cunningham. A shout goes out as well to Laura Daly, Brett Palana-Shanahan, Meredith O'Hayre, Rachel Engelson, and Sue Beale.

And lest I forget, I'd like to thank all the local espresso shops and the entire cast of *South Park* for keeping me awake and laughing throughout this process.

—*Barb Karg*

Introduction

THROUGHOUT HISTORY women have never lacked in their opinions of men. Let's face it; the mere thought that woman actually evolved from man isn't always an easy pill to swallow. But despite humble beginnings, women quickly proved to be a tour de force of mystery and mayhem inflicted on the male kingdom. Queen Victoria thought men selfish and miserable. Erica Jong felt the male/female mix would never work. Marilyn Monroe thought diamonds were a girl's best friend.

Women go shopping. Men start wars. Cornered by a plenitude of feminine wiles, men have been forced to rethink their personal and professional strategies. Yet despite their faults or perhaps because of them, women still love men no matter if their statements belie that belief. The battle of the sexes rages on as women continue to fight Napoleonic stigmas while at the same time shopping for the perfect pair of stilettos.

Macho may not be "mucho," but at the end of the day, the female species will slip between the sheets and ponder what life would be like without all the Adams of the world.

"   "
. . .

Sometimes I wonder if men and women really suit each other. Perhaps they should live next door and just visit now and then.

~ *Katharine Hepburn*

Men and women, women and men. It will never work.

~ *Erica Jong*

Marriage—a book of which the first chapter is written in poetry and the remaining chapters in prose.

~ *Beverley Nichols*

To be successful, a woman has to be much better at her job than a man.

~ *Golda Meir*

One advantage of marriage is that, when you fall out of love with him or he falls out of love with you, it keeps you together until you fall in again.

~ *Judith Viorst*

How absurd and delicious it is to be in love with somebody younger than yourself. Everybody should try it.

~ *Barbara Pym*

I adore him . . . I have never been so happy. I have real love.

~ *Princess Diana*

I'm female, thank God, because if I was male this really would be difficult. And, of course, I don't attempt to sound like my father—I do my own thing.

~ *Lisa Marie Presley*

The average man is more interested in a woman who is interested in him than he is in a woman with beautiful legs.

~ *Marlene Dietrich*

I'd marry again if I found a man who had fifteen million dollars, would sign over half to me, and guarantee that he'd be dead within a year.

~ *Bette Davis*

Men are like a deck of cards.
You'll find the occasional
king, but most are jacks.

⌒ Laura Swenson

Women must try to do things
as men have tried. When they
fail their failure must be but
a challenge to others.

⌒ Amelia Earhart

A simple enough pleasure, surely,
to have breakfast alone with one's
husband, but how seldom married
people in the midst of life achieve it.

⌒ Anne Spencer Morrow Lindbergh

If you never want to see a man again say, "I love you, I want to marry you, I want to have children." They leave skid marks.

~ *Rita Rudner*

I have met few men in my life, worth repeating eight times.

~ *Elizabeth Cady Stanton*

A successful man is one who makes more money than his wife can spend. A successful woman is one who can find such a man.

~ *Lana Turner*

Once in his life, every man is entitled to fall madly in love with a gorgeous redhead.

~ *Lucille Ball*

Saudi Arabian police arrested seven teenage boys for leering at women. In accordance with Saudi law, the boys will be whipped and the women will be stoned to death.

~ *Tina Fey*

If men could menstruate . . . clearly, menstruation would become an enviable, boast-worthy, masculine event: Men would brag about how long and how much . . . . Sanitary supplies would be federally funded and free. Of course, some men would still pay for the prestige of such commercial brands as Paul Newman Tampons, Muhammed Ali's Rope-a-Dope Pads, John Wayne Maxi Pads, and Joe Namath Jock Shields: "For Those Light Bachelor Days."

~ *Gloria Steinem*

Men make the moral code and
they expect women to accept it.

~ *Emmeline Parkhurst*

**Boy George is all
England needs, another
queen who can't dress.**

~ *Joan Rivers*

I resent men who are afraid of women's strength.

—*Anais Nin*

If men could get pregnant,
abortion would be a sacrament.

~ *Florynce R. Kennedy*

A girl can wait for the right man to come along but in the meantime that still doesn't mean she can't have a wonderful time with all the wrong ones.

~ *Cher*

Men never believe a woman can do anything.

~ *Christina Stead*

My father was very strong. I don't agree with a lot of the ways he brought me up. I don't agree with a lot of his values, but he did have a lot of integrity, and if he told us not to do something, he didn't do it either.

~ *Madonna*

**Women are superior to men.
I don't even think we're equal.**

~ *Barbra Streisand*

When you see what some girls
marry, you realize how much they
must hate to work for a living.

~ *Helen Rowland*

**The longer I'm around a man, the more
likely he is to try something funny. Like
they always say, familiarity breeds attempt.**

~ *Jayne Mansfield*

**Ten men waiting for me
at the door? Send one of
them home, I'm tired.**

~ *Mae West*

There are big men, men of intellect, intellectual men, men of talent and men of action; but the great man is difficult to find, and it needs— apart from discernment— a certain greatness to find him.

~ *Margot Asquith*

Men always fall for frigid women because they put on the best show.

~ *Fanny Brice*

Before marriage, a girl has to make love to a man to hold him. After marriage, she has to hold him to make love to him.

~ *Marilyn Monroe*

If you want anything said, ask a man. If you want anything done, ask a woman.

~ *Margaret Thatcher*

When a man can't explain a woman's actions, the first thing he thinks about is the condition of her uterus.

~ *Clare Booth Luce*

If men got pregnant, there would be safe, reliable methods of birth control. They'd be inexpensive, too.

~ *Anna Quindlen*

**Now men and women are separate
and unequal. We should be hand
in hand; in fact, we should have
our arms around each other.**

~ *Cloris Leachman*

Man reaches the highest point of
lovableness at twelve to seventeen—
to get it back, in a second flowering,
at the age of seventy to ninety.

~ *Isak Dinesen*

**I think every woman
is entitled to a middle
husband she can forget.**

~ *Adela Rogers St. John*

Men weren't really the enemy—they were fellow victims suffering from an outmoded masculine mystique that made them feel unnecessarily inadequate when there were no bears to kill.

~ *Betty Friedan*

I have never borne a grudge against any man whom I've loved. All the men I've had in my life are unique and irreplaceable.

~ *Catherine Deneuve*

Men are all right for friends, but as soon as you marry them they turn into cranky old fathers, even the wild ones. They begin to tell you what's sensible and what's foolish, and want you to stick at home all the time. I prefer to be foolish when I feel like it, and be accountable to nobody.

~ *Willa Cather*

Upscale young men seem to go for the kind of woman who plays with a full deck of credit cards, who won't cry when she's knocked to the ground while trying to board the six o'clock Eastern shuttle, and whose schedule doesn't allow for a sexual encounter lasting more than twelve minutes.

~ *Barbara Ehrenreich*

O! if those selfish men—who are the cause of all one's misery, only knew what their poor slaves go through! What suffering—what humiliation to the delicate feelings of a poor woman, above all a young one—especially with those nasty doctors.

〜 *Queen Victoria*

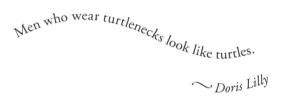

Men who wear turtlenecks look like turtles.

〜 *Doris Lilly*

I am a marvelous house-keeper. Every time I leave a man I keep his house.

〜 *Zsa Zsa Gabor*

Three wise men of Gotham
Went to sea in a bowl;
If the bowl had been stronger,
My story would have been longer.

∼ *Mother Goose*

**Destiny is something men
select; women achieve
it only by default or
stupendous suffering.**

∼ *Harriet Rosenstein*

**It was the men I deceived the
most that I loved the most.**

∼ *Marguerite Duras*

The history of men's opposition
to women's emancipation
is more interesting perhaps
than the story of that
emancipation itself.

~ *Virginia Woolf*

Don't accept rides
from strange men, and
remember that all men
are as strange as hell.

~ *Robin Morgan*

If all the rich men in the world divided
up their money amongst themselves,
there wouldn't be enough to go round.

~ *Christina Stead*

I know a lot of wonderful men married to pills, and I know a lot of pills married to wonderful women. So one shouldn't judge that way.

~ *Barbara Bush*

I don't like the typical good-looking guy. I know this sounds ridiculous, but I like guys with love handles. When he doesn't care 100 percent about his body, I don't have to obsess about mine. I hate a washboard stomach—does not turn me on.

~ *Tara Reid*

Why get married and make one man miserable when I can stay single and make thousands miserable?

~ *Carrie Snow*

Someone asked me why women don't gamble as much as men do, and I gave the commonsensical reply that we don't have as much money. That was a true and incomplete answer. In fact, women's total instinct for gambling is satisfied by marriage.

~ *Gloria Steinem*

My husband and I didn't sign a pre-nuptial agreement. We signed a mutual suicide pact.

~ *Roseanne Barr*

To the man who only has a hammer, everything he encounters begins to look like a nail.

~ *Jane Fonda*

I'd like to introduce someone who has just come into my life. I've admired him for thirty-five years. He's someone who represents integrity, honesty, art, and on top of that stuff I'm actually sleeping with him.

~ *Shirley MacLaine*

Men think monogamy is something you make dining tables out of.

~ *Kathy Lette*

My ancestors wandered lost in the wilderness for forty years because even in biblical times, men would not stop to ask for directions.

⁓ *Elayne Boosler*

I gave my beauty and my youth to men. I am going to give my wisdom and experience to animals.

⁓ *Brigitte Bardot*

Beware of men who cry. It's true that men who cry are sensitive and in touch with their feelings, but the only feelings they tend to be sensitive to and in touch with are their own.

⁓ *Nora Ephron*

If a man watches three football games in a row, he should be declared legally dead.

~ Erma Bombeck

Giving a man space is like giving a dog a computer: Chances are he will not use it wisely.

~ Bette-Jane Raphael

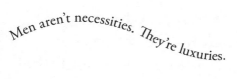

Men aren't necessities. They're luxuries.

~ Cher

When you lie down with dogs, you get up with fleas.

~ Jean Harlow

Woman might be able to fake orgasms. But man can fake whole relationships.

~ *Sharon Stone*

Men are simple things. They can survive a whole weekend with only three things: beer, boxer shorts and batteries for the remote control.

~ *Diana Jordan*

Can you imagine a world without men? No crime and lots of happy fat women.

~ *Nicole Hollander*

Never date a man whose belt buckle is bigger than his head.

~ *Brett Butler*

For a certain type of woman who risks losing her identity in a man, there are all those questions . . . until you get to the point and know that you really are living a love story.

~ *Anouk Aimee*

So far I've always kept my diet secret, but now I might as well tell everyone what it is: Lots of grapefruit throughout the day and plenty of virile young men.

~ *Angie Dickinson*

Personally, I think if a woman hasn't met the right man by the time she's twenty-four, she may be lucky.

~ *Deborah Kerr*

The scorn men express for a male who does housework is exceeded only by their aversion to a woman who doesn't.

~ Penny Kome

If a man talks bad about all women, it usually means he was burned by one woman.

~ Coco Chanel

Women want mediocre men, and men are working to be as mediocre as possible.

~ Margaret Mead

Women's liberation is just a lot of foolishness. It's men who are discriminated against. They can't bear children. And no one is likely to do anything about that.

~ *Golda Meir*

American husbands are the best in the world; no other husbands are so generous to their wives, or can be so easily divorced.

~ *Elinor Glyn*

Women complain about sex more often than men. Their gripes fall into two major categories: (1) Not enough. (2) Too much.

~ *Ann Landers*

Men who think that a woman's past love affairs lessen her love for them are usually stupid and weak. A woman can bring a new love to each man she loves, providing there are not too many.

~ *Marilyn Monroe*

I don't think a powerful man would be interesting unless he'd be nice, attractive, with or without the power. Men are interested in powerful men. Women are interested in terrific men!

~ *Dorothy Stratten*

Some husbands are living proof that a woman can take a joke.

~ *Anonymous*

Men who care passionately for women attach themselves at least as much to the temple and to the accessories of the cult as to their goddess herself.

~ *Marguerite Yourcenar*

I suppose when they reach a certain age some men are afraid to grow up. It seems the older the men get, the younger their new wives get.

~ *Elizabeth Taylor*

Women speak because they wish to speak, whereas a man speaks only when driven to speech by something outside himself—like, for instance, he can't find any clean socks.

~ *Jean Kerr*

I love men, even though they're lying, cheating scumbags.

~ *Gwyneth Paltrow*

I would rather be a beggar and single than a queen and married.

~ *Queen Elizabeth I*

A lot of guys think the larger a woman's breasts are, the less intelligent she is. I don't think it works like that. I think it's the opposite. I think the larger a woman's breasts are, the less intelligent the men become.

~ *Anita Wise*

I've been on so many
blind dates, I should
get a free dog.

~ Wendy Liebman

A woman's rule of thumb: if it
has tires or testicles, you're going
to have trouble with it.

~ Unknown

Beauty is in the eye of the
beholder and it may be
necessary from time to time to
give a stupid or misinformed
beholder a black eye.

~ Miss Piggy

Men are irrelevant.

~ *Fay Weldon*

If you talk about yourself, he'll think you're boring. If you talk about others, he'll think you're a gossip. If you talk about him, he'll think you're a brilliant conversationalist.

~ *Linda Sunshine*

Men, being conditioned badly, are always feeling nooses closing around their necks, even dumpy boors no girl would take on a bet.

~ *Cynthia Heimel*

This guy says, "I'm perfect for you, because I'm a cross between a macho and a sensitive man."
I said, "Oh, a gay trucker?"

~ *Judy Tenuta*

I've dated men my age, younger than me and older. The only difference is the young ones are quicker at taking out the garbage.

~ *Lara Flynn Boyle*

When a man brings his wife flowers for no reason, there's a reason.

~ *Molly McGee*

An archaeologist is the best husband a woman can have. The older she gets, the more interested he is in her.

~ Agatha Christie

It is the loose ends with which men hang themselves.

~ Zelda Fitzgerald

Our struggle today is not to have a female Einstein get appointed as an assistant professor. It is for a woman schlemiel to get as quickly promoted as a male schlemiel.

~ Bella Abzug

**The male is a domestic animal
which, if treated with firmness, can
be trained to do most things.**

~ *Jilly Cooper*

Men make love more
intensely at twenty,
but make love better,
however, at thirty.

~ *Catherine II of Russia*

Never refer to any part of his body
below the waist as "cute" or "little";
never expects him to do anything
about birth control; never ask if he
changes his sheets occasionally; never
request that he sleep in the wet spot.

~ *C. E. Crimmins*

Getting along with men isn't what's truly important. The vital knowledge is how to get along with a man. One man.

~ *Phyllis McGinley*

If love means never having to say you're sorry, then marriage means always having to say everything twice. Husbands, due to an unknown quirk of the universe, never hear you the first time.

~ **Estelle Getty**

If your husband and a lawyer were drowning and you had to choose, would you go to lunch or to a movie?

~ *Unknown*

Every woman must admit, and every man with as much sense as a woman, that it's very hard to make a home for any man if he's always in it.

~ *Winifred Kirkland*

Husbands are awkward things to deal with; even keeping them in hot water will not make them tender.

~ *Mary Buckley*

When men reach their sixties and retire, they go to pieces. Women go right on cooking.

~ *Gail Sheehy*

What is most beautiful in virile men is something feminine; what is most beautiful in feminine women is something masculine.

〜 *Susan Sontag*

My husband and I divorced over religious differences. He thought he was God, and I didn't.

〜 *Author Unknown*

Male and female represent the two sides of the great radical dualism. But in fact they are perpetually passing into one another. Fluid hardens to solid, solid rushes to fluid. There is no wholly masculine man, no purely feminine woman.

〜 *Margaret Fuller*

When I eventually met Mr. Right I had no idea that his first name was Always.

~ Rita Rudner

The memory of most men is an abandoned cemetery where lie, unsung and unhonored, the dead whom they have ceased to cherish. Any lasting grief is reproof to their forgetfulness.

~ Marguerite Yourcenar

On the whole, I haven't found men unduly loath to say, "I love you." The real trick is to get them to say, "Will you marry me?"

~ Ilka Chase

You people married to Italian men, you know what it's like.

〜 *Geraldine Ferraro*

Too often the great decisions are originated and given form in bodies made up wholly of men, or so completely dominated by them that whatever of special value women have to offer is shunted aside without expression.

〜 *Eleanor Roosevelt*

If you're considered a beauty, it's hard to be accepted doing anything but standing around.

〜 *Cybill Shepherd*

I married a German. Every night I dress up as Poland and he invades me.

~ *Bette Midler*

Show me a woman who doesn't feel guilt and I'll show you a man.

~ *Erica Jong*

Whenever you want to marry someone, go have lunch with his ex-wife.

~ *Shelley Winters*

Whatever women do they must do twice as well as men to be thought half as good. Luckily, this is not difficult.

~ *Charlotte Whitton*

The people I'm getting furious with are the women's liberationists. They keep getting on their soapboxes proclaiming that women are brighter than men. That's true, but it should be kept quiet or it ruins the whole racket.

〜 *Anita Loos*

The main difference between men and women is that men are lunatics and women are idiots.

〜 *Rebecca West*

If men can run the world, why can't they stop wearing neckties? How intelligent is it to start the day by tying a little noose around your neck?

~ *Linda Ellerbee*

How wrong it is for a woman to expect the man to build the world she wants, rather than to create it herself.

~ *Anais Nin*

I don't need a man. But I'm happier with one. I like to have someone I can touch and squeeze and kiss. But I don't fold up and die if I don't have a man around.

~ *Cher*

I think men are afraid to be with a successful woman, because we are terribly strong, we know what we want and we are not fragile enough.

∼ *Shirley Bassey*

Most of us women like men, you know; it's just that we find them a constant disappointment.

∼ *Clare Short*

Scratch a king and find a fool!

∼ *Dorothy Parker*

If high heels were so wonderful, men would be wearing them.

∼ *Sue Grafton*

A woman has got to love a bad man once or twice in her life, to be thankful for a good one.

~ *Marjorie Kinnan Rawlings*

Why is it that men can be bastards and women must wear pearls and smile?

~ *Lynn Hecht Schafren*

I need someone physically stronger than me . . . I am always on top. It's really unfortunate. I am begging for the man that can put me on the bottom. Or the woman. Anybody that can take me down.

~ *Angelina Jolie*

Find me a man who's interesting
enough to have dinner
with and I'll be happy.

~ *Lauren Bacall*

Men have been trained and
conditioned by women, not
unlike the way Pavlov conditioned
his dogs, into becoming their
slaves. As compensation for their
labours men are given periodic
use of a woman's vagina.

~ *Esther Vilar*

God made man stronger but not necessarily more intelligent. He gave women intuition and femininity. And, used properly, that combination easily jumbles the brain of any man I've ever met.

~ *Farrah Fawcett*

Man is defined as a human being and a woman as a female—whenever she behaves as a human being she is said to imitate the male.

~ *Simone de Beauvoir*

When a woman reaches orgasm with a man she is only collaborating with the patriarchal system, eroticizing her own oppression.

~ *Sheila Jeffrys*

Changing husbands is only changing troubles.

~ *Kathleen Norris*

The first time you buy a house you think how pretty it is and sign the check. The second time you look to see if the basement has termites. It's the same with men.

~ *Lupe Velez*

Any intelligent woman who reads the marriage contract, and then goes into it, deserves all the consequences.

~ *Isadora Duncan*

Man forgives woman anything save the wit to outwit him.

~ *Minna Antrim*

Fighting is essentially a masculine idea; a woman's weapon is her tongue.

~ *Hermione Gingold*

There's a place for corporate wives, but there's no place for corporate husbands.

~ *Karen Valenstein*

I married beneath me. All women do.

~ *Nancy Astor*

How different the reasoning is that men adopt when they are discussing the cases of men and those of women.

~ *Emmeline Pankhurst*

I wish that men were as
resolute as women.

~ *Anne Javouhey*

When I'm out with my
girlfriends at the bar, and
I see some young eighteen-
year-old boy, just for fun
I say, "Hi honey. Do you
like girls? Do you like girls
exclusively? Oh, good."

~ *Yasmine Bleeth*

Macho does not
prove mucho.

~ *Zsa Zsa Gabor*

The quickest way to a man's heart is through his chest.

~ *Roseanne Barr*

There are times not to flirt. When you're sick. When you're with children. When you're on the witness stand.

~ *Joyce Jillson*

It is not her body that he wants but it is only through her body that he can take possession of another human being, so he must labor upon her body, he must enter her body, to make his claim.

~ *Joyce Carol Oates*

Many of our troubles in the world today arise from an over-emphasis of the masculine, and a neglect of the feminine. This modern world is an aggressive, hyperactive, competitive, masculine world, and it needs the woman's touch as never before.

~ *Eva Burrows*

A gentleman is simply a patient wolf.

~ *Lana Turner*

We have reason to believe that man first walked upright to free his hands for masturbation.

~ *Lily Tomlin*

It is a truth universally acknowledged that a single man in possession of a good fortune must be in want of a wife.

~ *Jane Austen*

Whether women are better than men I cannot say, but I can say they are certainly no worse.

~ *Golda Meir*

Bloody men are like bloody buses—you wait for about a year and as soon as one approaches your stop two or three others appear.

~ *Wendy Cope*

If it's true that men are such beasts, this must account for the fact that most women are animal lovers.

~ *Doris Day*

If it weren't for women, men would still be wearing last week's socks.

~ *Cynthia Nelms*

Woman is the dominant sex. Men have to do all sorts of stuff to prove that they are worthy of woman's attention.

~ *Camille Paglia*

We still think of a powerful man as a born leader and a powerful woman as an anomaly.

~ *Margaret Atwood*

Instead of getting hard ourselves and trying to compete, women should try to give their best qualities to men—bring them softness, teach them how to cry.

~ *Joan Baez*

A woman's head is always influenced by heart; but a man's heart by his head.

~ *Lady Marguerite Blessington*

I blame my mother for my poor sex life. All she told me was, "the man goes on top and the woman underneath." For three years my husband and I slept on bunk beds.

~ *Joan Rivers*

Women see better than men. Men see lazily, if they do not expect to act. Women see quite without any wish to act.

~ *Jane Goodsell*

Guys are like roses. You've got to watch out for the pricks.

~ *Unknown*

The woman's vision is deep reaching, the man's far reaching. With the man the world is his heart, with the woman the heart is her world.

~ *Betty Grable*

Marriage is a great institution, but who wants to live in an institution?

~ *Katharine Hepburn*

Do not put such unlimited power into the hands of husbands. Remember all men would be tyrants if they could.

~ *Abigail Adams*

The only time a woman really succeeds in changing a man is when he's a baby.

~ *Natalie Wood*

When he's late for dinner, I know
he's either having an affair
or is lying dead in the street.
I always hope it's the street.

~ *Jessica Tandy*

I love the male body,
it's better designed
than the male mind.

~ *Andrea Newman*

It is a man's world, and you men can have it.

~ *Katherine Anne Porter*

To call a man an animal is to flatter
him; he's a machine, a walking dildo.

~ *Valerie Solanis*

My boyfriend and I live together, which means we don't have sex—ever. Now that the milk is free, we've both become lactose intolerant.

~ *Margaret Cho*

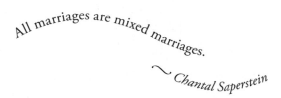

All marriages are mixed marriages.

~ *Chantal Saperstein*

I've no time for broads who want to rule the world alone. Without men, who'd do up the zipper on the back of your dress?

~ **Bette Davis**

A man's home may seem to be his castle on the outside; inside is more often his nursery.

~ *Clare Booth Luce*

I admit, I have a tremendous sex drive.
My boyfriend lives forty miles away.

~ *Phyllis Diller*

If all men are born free, why is it that all women are born slaves?

~ *Mary Astell*

A man is an accessory, like a pair of earrings. It may finish the outfit, but you don't really need it to keep you warm.

~ *Rosemary Mittlemark*

What's all this crap about finding the perfect man? I'd settle for one who has his own car and a steady job.

~ *Mary Rockne*

I think it's about time we voted for senators with breasts. After all, we've been voting for boobs long enough.

~ *Claire Sargent*

I had only one beau in Altoona: a dentist. For a while I dreamed about what marriage to him would be like. But I stopped dreaming one Saturday when we went picnicking and I saw him in a bathing suit. He was covered all over with fur and reminded me of an orangutan.

~ *Hedda Hopper*

I fear nothing as much as a man who is witty all day long.

~ *Madame de Sevigne*

Like many other women, I could not
understand why every man who has
changed a diaper has felt impelled,
in recent years, to write about it.

~ Barbara Ehrenreich

The best way to get most husbands
to do something is to suggest that
perhaps they are too old to do it.

~ Anne Bancroft

I love the lines the men use to get us
into bed. "Please, I'll only put it in for
a minute." What am I, a microwave?

~ Beverly Mickins

You can always spot a well-informed man—his views are the same as yours.

~ *Ilka Chase*

The bicycle is just as good company as most husbands and, when it gets old and shabby, a woman can dispose of it and get a new one without shocking the entire community.

~ *Ann Strong*

I have wallowed with the vermin, so I know men's minds.

~ *Mother Jones*

Not only is it harder to be a man, it is also harder to become one.

~ *Arianna Stassinopoulos*

My theory is that men are no more liberated than women.

~ *Indira Gandhi*

Sometimes I think if there was a third sex men wouldn't get so much as a glance from me.

~ *Amanda Vail*

No nice men are good at getting taxis.

~ *Katherine Whitehorn*

How can a man marry wisely in his twenties? The girl he's going to wind up wanting hasn't even been born.

~ *Mignon McLaughlin*

I wonder why men get serious at all. They have this delicate, long thing hanging outside their bodies which goes up and down by its own will. If I were a man I would always be laughing at myself.

~ *Yoko Ono*

Beware of the man who loves his mother's macaroni and cheese more than he loves sex. Or you. Or anything.

~ *Linda Stasi*

I didn't want five husbands, but it happened that way and that's all there is to it.

~ *Rita Hayworth*

A painting is like a man. If you can live without it, there isn't much point in having it.

~ Lila Acheson Wallace

Honey, I don't care what Hollywood says . . . real men prefer real breasts.

~ Kathy Shaskan

I don't have a problem with men. I have a problem with stupid men.

~ Maggie Estep

The usual masculine grace has long been a thorn in my flesh. The rooster may do the crowing, but it is the faithful hen who lays the eggs.

~ Elizabeth Cady Stanton

When you meet a man, don't you always idly wonder what he'd be like in bed? I do.

~ *Helen Gurley Brown*

Show me a frigid women and, nine times out of ten, I'll show you a little man.

~ *Julie Burchill*

Before marriage, a man will lay down his life for you; after marriage he won't even lay down his newspaper.

~ *Helen Rowland*

A man would prefer to come home to an unmade bed and a happy woman than to a neatly made bed and an angry woman.

~ *Marlene Dietrich*

Men aren't the way they are because they want to drive women crazy; they've been trained to be that way for thousands of years. And that training makes it very difficult for men to be intimate.

~ *Barbara De Angelis*

The more I see of men, the more I like dogs.

~ *Madame de Staël*

The trouble with some women is that they get all excited about nothing—and then marry him.

~ *Cher*

Woman's virtue is man's greatest invention.

~ *Cornelia Otis Skinner*

The best contraceptive is the word no—repeated frequently.

~ *Margaret Smith*

If it wasn't for women men would still be hanging from trees.

~ *Marilyn Peterson*

I think women have an innate ability to be intuitive with people that they truly love, but they have to trust that inner voice, and I think it is there. I think we are more intuitive than men.

~ *Andie MacDowell*

You know why God is a man? Because if God was a woman she would have made sperm taste like chocolate.

~ *Carrie Snow*

Men say they love independence in a woman, but they don't waste a second demolishing it brick by brick.

~ **Candice Bergen**

A woman's always younger than a man of equal years.

~ *Elizabeth Barrett Browning*

You never see a man walking down the street with a woman who has a little potbelly and a bald spot.

~ *Elayne Boosler*

All men are not slimy warthogs. Some men are silly giraffes, some woebegone puppies, some insecure frogs. But if one is not careful, those slimy warthogs can ruin it for all the others.

~ *Cynthia Heimel*

If men had more up top we'd need less up front.

~ *Jaci Stephen*

What's with you men? Would hair stop growing on your chest if you asked directions somewhere?

~ *Erma Bombeck*

If the world were a logical place, men would ride side saddle.

~ *Rita Mae Brown*

A man is two people, himself and his cock. A man always takes his friend to the party. Of the two, the friend is the nicer, being more able to show his feelings.

~ *Beryl Bainbridge*

In the silence of night I have often wished for just a few words of love from one man, rather than the applause of thousands of people.

~ *Judy Garland*

Men are no more immune from emotions than women; we think women are more emotional because the culture lets them give free vent to certain feelings, feminine ones, that is, no anger please, but it's okay to turn on the waterworks.

~ *Una Stannard*

If the bedroom were a kitchen, women would be crockpots and men would be microwaves.

~ *Diana Jordan*

Men are nicotine-soaked, beer-besmirched, whiskey-greased, red-eyed devils.

~ *Carry Nation*

Talking with a man is like trying to saddle a cow. You work like hell, but what's the point?

~ *Gladys Upham*

Don't let a man put anything over on you except an umbrella.

~ *Mae West*

A woman's a woman until the day she dies, but a man's a man only as long as he can.

~ *Moms Mabley*

The lovely thing about being forty is that you can appreciate twenty-five-year-old men.

~ *Colleen McCullough*

I would like it if men had to partake in the same hormonal cycles to which we're subjected monthly. Maybe that's why men declare war—because they have a need to bleed on a regular basis.

~ *Brett Butler*

When a woman is very, very bad,
she is awful, but when a man is
correspondingly good, he is weird.

~ *Minna Antrim*

There were three of us
in this marriage, so it
was a bit crowded.

~ *Princess Diana*

Why do we let men
upset us so much? They
can't perpetuate the
species without us! We've
got the upper hand!

~ *Stephanie Piro*

Like every good little feminist-in-training in the sixties, I burned my bra—and now . . . I realize [that bra] supported me better than any man I'd ever known.

~ *Susan Sweetzer*

I've finally figured out that being male is the same thing, more or less, as having a personality disorder.

~ *Carol Shields*

There is so little difference between husbands you might as well keep the first.

~ *Adela Rogers St. Johns*

I've been married to one
Marxist and one Fascist,
and neither one would
take the garbage out.

~ Lee Grant

**I usually make up my mind about a man in
ten seconds, and I very rarely change it.**

~ Margaret Thatcher

A father is always making
his baby into a little woman.
And when she is a woman
he turns her back again.

~ Enid Bagnold

Is it better for a woman to marry a man
who loves her than a man she loves?

~ Amy Bloom

It seems as though women keep growing. Eventually they can have little or nothing in common with the men they chose long ago.

~ *Eugenie Clark*

What a man sows, that shall he and his relations reap.

~ *Clarissa Graves*

Because I am a woman, I must make unusual efforts to succeed. If I fail, no one will say, "She doesn't have what it takes." They will say, "Women don't have what it takes."

~ *Clare Boothe Luce*

Before we make love my husband takes a pain killer.

~ *Joan Rivers*

I have always dressed according to certain Basic Guy Fashion Rules, including:
* Both of your socks should always be the same color
* Or they should at least both be fairly dark.

~ *Jilly Cooper*

Whatever they may be in public life, whatever their relations with men, in their relations with women, all men are rapists and that's all they are. They rape us with their eyes, their laws, their codes.

~ *Marilyn French*

They say marriage is a contract. No, it's not. Contracts come with warranties. When something goes wrong, you can take it back to the manufacturer. If your husband starts acting up, you can't take him back to his mama's house: "I don't know; he just stopped working. He's just lying around making this funny noise."

~ *Wanda Sykes*

A man's got to do what a man's got to do. A woman must do what he can't.

~ *Rhonda Hansome*

A nymphomaniac is a women as obsessed with sex as the average man.

~ *Mignon McLaughlin*

I never married because there was no need. I have three pets at home, which answer the same purpose as a husband. I have a dog which growls every morning, a parrot which swears all afternoon and a cat that comes home late at night.

~ *Marie Corelli*

Man, born of woman, has found it a hard thing to forgive her for giving him birth. The patriarchal protest against the ancient matriarch has borne strange fruit through the years.

~ *Lillian Smith*

I have always been principally interested in men for sex. I've always thought any sane woman would be a lover of women because loving men is such a mess. I have always wished I'd fall in love with a woman. Damn.

~ *Germaine Greer*

Where women love each other, men learn to smother their mutual dislike.

~ *George Eliot*

My fiancee and I are having a little disagreement. What I want is a big church wedding with bridesmaids and flowers and a no expense spared reception; and what he wants is to break off our engagement.

~ *Sally Poplin*

My ultimate fantasy is to entice a man to my bedroom, put a gun to his head and say, "Make babies or die."

~ *Ruby Wax*

No matter how love-sick a woman is, she shouldn't take the first pill that comes along.

~ *Joyce Brothers*

It would be a thousand pities if women wrote like men, or lived like men, or looked like men, for if two sexes are quite inadequate, considering the vastness and variety of the world, how should we manage with one only?

~ *Virginia Woolf*

Behind every successful man
is a surprised woman.

~ *Maryon Pearson*

He's just a rhinestone in the rough.

~ *Dorothy Parker*

Arthur Miller wouldn't have married me if I had been nothing but a dumb blonde.

~ *Marilyn Monroe*

A dress makes no sense unless it inspires men to want to take it off you.

~ *Francoise Sagan*

You don't want to have to be the man and the woman in the relationship. I always say you want a man who can fix the toilet.

~ *Pamela Anderson*

Men know they are sexual exiles. They wander the earth seeking satisfaction, craving and despising, never content. There is nothing in that anguished motion for women to envy.

~ *Camille Paglia*

Women are not forgiven for aging. Robert Redford's lines of distinction are my old-age wrinkles.

~ *Jane Fonda*

The beauty myth moves for men as a mirage; its power lies in its ever-receding nature. When the gap is closed, the lover embraces only his own disillusion.

~ *Naomi Wolf*

There are plenty of men who philander during the summer, to be sure, but they are usually the same lot who philander during the winter—albeit with less convenience.

~ *Nora Ephron*

Why did God create men? Because vibrators can't mow the lawn.

~ *Madonna*

When women are
depressed, they eat
or go shopping. Men
invade another country.
It's a whole different
way of thinking.

~ *Elayne Boosler*

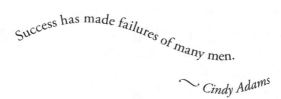

Success has made failures of many men.

~ *Cindy Adams*

Men are too emotional to vote. Their
conduct at baseball games and political
conventions shows this, while their innate
tendency to appeal to force renders them
particularly unfit for the task of government.
. . . Man's place is in the armory.

~ *Alive Duer Miller*

I never liked the men I loved, and never loved the men I liked.

~ *Fanny Brice*

Human sexuality has been regulated and shaped by men to serve men's needs.

~ *Ana Castillo*

I've gone for each type: the rough guy; the nerdy, sweet, lovable guy; and the slick guy. I don't really have a type. Men in general are a good thing.

~ *Jennifer Aniston*

It was a mixed marriage. I'm human, he was a Klingon.

~ *Carol Leifer*

Men are much simpler mechanisms than women. Nothing changes them. . . . Even when they have a midlife crisis, they do it in a mindless way. That's why I think we should let men go off and have affairs and drive fast cars and dream of being virile—and we should run the world.

~ *Goldie Hawn*

Men are those creatures with two legs and eight hands.

~ *Jayne Mansfield*

Once a man is on hand, a woman tends to stop believing in her own beliefs.

~ *Colette Dowling*

I married the first man I ever kissed.
When I tell this to my children
they just about throw up.

～ *Barbara Bush*

It isn't always easy seeing your
boyfriend, like, you know,
in a bathtub with some girl
or kissing some other girl.

～ *Reese Witherspoon*

I've met a lot of hard-boiled eggs in my
time, but you, you're twenty minutes.

～ *Jan Sterling*

A woman who thinks she
is intelligent demands the
same rights as man. An
intelligent woman gives up.

～ *Sidonie Gabrielle Colette*

I turned down a date once because I was looking for someone a little closer to the top of the food chain.

~ *Judy Tenuta*

If it's a woman, it's caustic; if it's a man, it's authoritative.

~ *Barbara Walters*

Men make angry music and it's called rock-and-roll; women include anger in their vocabulary and suddenly they're angry and militant.

~ *Ani DiFranco*

He is every other inch a gentleman.

~ *Rebecca West*

You can seduce a man without taking anything off, without even touching him.

~ *Rae Dawn Chong*

The average man has a carefully cultivated ignorance about household matters—from what to do with the crumbs to the grocer's telephone number—a sort of cheerful inefficiency which protects him.

~ *Crystal Eastman*

Some men are so macho they'll get you pregnant just to kill a rabbit.

~ *Maureen Murphy*

Men for the sake of getting a living forget to live.

~ *Margaret Fuller*

Every time a man expects, as he says, his money to work for him, he is expecting other people to work for him.

~ *Dorothy L. Sayers*

One difference between a man
and a machine is that a machine
is quiet when well-oiled.

~ *Anonymous*

Any woman who still thinks marriage is a fifty-fifty proposition is only proving that she doesn't understand either men or percentages.

~ *Rose F. Kennedy*

I've only slept with men I've been married to. How many women can make that claim?

~ *Elizabeth Taylor*

A lover may be a shadowy creature, but husbands are made of flesh and blood.

~ *Amy Levy*

Men have laid down the rules and definitions by which the world is run, and one of the objects of their definitions is woman.

~ *Sally Kempton*

Men were made for war.
Without it they wandered
greyly about, getting under
the feet of the women, who
were trying to organize the
really important things of life.

~ *Alice Thomas Ellis*

I say I don't sleep with
married men, but what
I mean is that I don't sleep
with happily married men.

~ *Britt Ekland*

You don't have to be married
to have a good friend as
your partner for life.

~ *Greta Garbo*

The male function is to produce sperm. We now have sperm banks.

~ *Valerie Solanis*

The tragedy of machismo is that a man is never quite man enough.

~ *Germaine Greer*

If you marry a man who cheats on his wife, you'll be married to a man who cheats on his wife.

~ *Ann Landers*

I only know that people call me a feminist whenever I express sentiments that differentiate me from a doormat or a prostitute.

~ *Rebecca West*

When a woman behaves like a man, why doesn't she behave like a nice man?

~ *Dame Edith Evans*

A woman voting for divorce is like a turkey voting for Christmas.

~ *Alice Glynn*

People don't have fortunes left them in that style nowadays; men have to work and women to marry for money. It's a dreadfully unjust world.

~ *Louisa May Alcott*

Only time can heal your broken heart, just as only time can heal his broken arms and legs.

~ *Miss Piggy*

If love is the answer, could you please rephrase the question?

~ Lily Tomlin

God created men, but I could do better.

~ Erma Bombeck

Men get opinions as boys learn to spell, By reiteration chiefly.

~ Elizabeth Barrett Browning

Husbands are like fires.
They go out if unattended.

~ Zsa Zsa Gabor

Gentleman: A man who buys two of the same morning paper from the doorman of his favorite nightclub when he leaves with his girl.

~ *Marlene Dietrich*

I like to wake up each morning feeling a new man.

~ *Jean Harlow*

Men have had every advantage of us in telling their own story. Education has been theirs in so much higher a degree; the pen has been in their hands. I will not allow books to prove any thing.

~ *Jane Austen*

I'm not always in that good with middle-aged heterosexual men.

~ *Kathy Griffin*

The prerequisite for making love is to like someone enormously.

~ *Helen Gurley Brown*

A male gynecologist is like an auto mechanic who never owned a car.

~ *Carrie Snow*

I'm married but the special man is my dog, Henry.

~ *Ana Gasteyer*

I don't understand it. Jack will spend any amount of money to buy votes, but he balks at investing a thousand dollars in a beautiful painting.

~ *Jackie Kennedy*

I dress for women and I undress for men.

~ *Angie Dickinson*

No one can make you feel inferior without your consent.

~ *Eleanor Roosevelt*

Whenever women catfight, men think it's going to turn to sex.

~ *Yasmine Bleeth*

The nice thing about egotists is that they don't talk about other people.

~ *Lucille S. Harper*

Men who want to support women in our struggle for freedom and justice should understand that it is not terrifically important to us that they learn to cry; it is important to us that they stop the crimes of violence against us.

~ *Andrea Dworkin*

Men are allowed to have passion and commitment for their work . . . a woman is allowed that feeling for a man, but not her work.

~ *Barbra Streisand*

Whatever you may look like, marry a man your own age—as your beauty fades, so will his eyesight.

~ *Phyllis Diller*

There are various orders of beauty, causing men to make fools of themselves in various styles.

~ *George Eliot*

Diamonds never leave you . . . men do!

~ *Shirley Bassey*

Why are women . . . so much more interesting to men than men are to women?

~ *Virginia Woolf*

Marrying a man is like buying something you've been admiring for a long time in a shop window. You may love it when you get it home, but it doesn't always go with everything else in the house.

~ *Jean Kerr*

We had a lot in common. I loved him and he loved him.

~ *Shelley Winters*

A woman isn't complete without a man. But where do you find a man—a real man—these days?

~ *Lauren Bacall*

Men seem unable to feel
equal to women: they must be
superior or they are inferior.

~ *Marilyn French*

My computer dating
bureau came up with a
perfect gentleman. Still,
I've got another three goes.

~ *Sally Poplin*

**There is nothing like a good
dose of another woman to make
a man appreciate his wife.**

~ *Clare Boothe Luce*

No one is more arrogant toward women,
more aggressive or scornful, than the
man who is anxious about his virility.

~ *Simone de Beauvoir*

I'm attracted to guys who are really confident and make conversation.

~ *Britney Spears*

How different the reasoning is that men adopt when they are discussing the cases of men and those of women.

~ *Emmeline Pankhurst*

Men are taught to apologize for their weaknesses, women for their strengths.

~ *Lois Wyse*

Women prefer men who have something tender about them—especially the legal kind.

~ *Kay Ingram*

Men like war: they do not hold much sway over birth, so they make up for it with death. Unlike women, men menstruate by shedding other people's blood.

~ *Lucy Ellman*

No man is responsible for his father. That was entirely his mother's affair.

~ *Margaret Turnbull*

Men define intelligence, men define usefulness, men tell us what is beautiful, men even tell us what is womanly.

~ *Sally Kempton*

A wedding is just like a funeral except that you get to smell your own flowers.

~ *Grace Hansen*

Men are like a fine wine. They all start out like grapes, and it's our job to stomp on them and keep them in the dark until they mature into something you'd like to have dinner with.

~ *Kathleen Mifsud*

Men know everything—all of them, all the time—no matter how stupid or inexperienced or arrogant or ignorant they are.

~ *Andrea Dworkin*

Men are beasts and even beasts don't behave as they do.

~ *Brigitte Bardot*

I'm a double bagger. Not only does my husband put a bag over my face when we're making love, but he also puts a bag over his head in case mine falls off.

~ *Joan Rivers*

We've chosen the path to equality, don't let them turn us around.

~ *Geraldine Ferraro*

As long as you know that most men are children, you know everything.

~ *Coco Chanel*

You see a lot of smart guys
with dumb women, but
you hardly ever see a smart
woman with a dumb guy.

~ Erica Jong

I'm a failure as a woman. My men
expect so much from me, because
of the image they've made of
me and that I've made of myself,
as a sex symbol. Men expect so
much, and I can't live up to it.

~ Marilyn Monroe

Women have got to make the world
safe for men since men have made
it so darned unsafe for women.

~ Lady Nancy Astor

Plain women know more about
men than beautiful ones do. But
beautiful women don't need to know
about men. It's the men who have
to know about beautiful women.

~ *Katherine Hepburn*

It isn't tying himself to
one woman that a man
dreads when he thinks of
marrying; it's separating
himself from all the others.

~ *Helen Rowland*

The best smell in the
world is that man
that you love.

~ *Jennifer Aniston*

The woman is the home. That's where she used to be, and that's where she still is. You might ask me, What if a man tries to be part of the home—will the woman let him? I answer yes. Because then he becomes one of the children.

~ *Marguerite Duras*

Sex is more fun than cars but cars refuel quicker than men.

~ *Germaine Greer*

The emotional, sexual, and psychological sterotyping of females begins when the doctor says, "It's a girl."

~ *Shirley Chisholm*

I don't have a boyfriend right now. I'm looking for anyone with a job that I don't have to support.

~ *Anna Nicole Smith*

Boys are sent out into the world to
buffet with its temptations,
to mingle with bad and good, to
govern and direct—girls are to dwell
in quiet homes among few friends,
to exercise a noiseless influence.

~ *Elizabeth Missing Sewell*

My husband said he wanted to have a relationship with a redhead, so I dyed my hair.

~ *Jane Fonda*

From the start, marriage was instituted for contemptible, practical reasons—an idea of men.

~ *Catherine Deneuve*

A guy is a lump like a doughnut. So, first you gotta get rid of all the stuff his mom did to him. And then you gotta get rid of all that macho crap that they pick up from beer commercials. And then there's my personal favorite, the male ego.

~ *Roseanne Barr*

Mountains appear more lofty the nearer they are approached, but great men resemble them not in this particular.

~ *Lady Marguerite Blessington*

There are few men more superstitious
than soldiers. They are, after all, the
men who live closest to death.

~ *Mary Stewart*

I require three things in a
man: He must be handsome,
ruthless, and stupid.

~ *Dorothy Parker*

Blessed is the man, who having
nothing to say, abstains from giving
wordy evidence of the fact.

~ *George Eliot*

Women are the only oppressed
group in our society that
lives in intimate association
with their oppressors.

~ *Evelyn Cunningham*

Husbands should be like Kleenex: soft, strong, and disposable.

~ *Madeline Kahn*

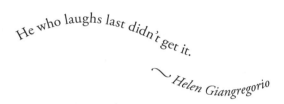

He who laughs last didn't get it.

~ *Helen Giangregorio*

The question arises as to whether it is possible not to live in the world of men and still to live in the world.

~ **Louise Bernikow**

All great men are gifted with intuition. They know without reasoning or analysis, what they need to know.

~ *Alexis Carrel*

In the United States adherence to the values of the masculine mystique makes intimate, self-revealing, deep friendships between men unusual.

— *Myriam Miedzian*

There is no female Mozart because there is no female Jack the Ripper.

— *Camille Paglia*

There are always women who will take men on their own terms. If I were a man I wouldn't bother to change while there are women like that around.

— *Ann Oakley*

A man that is ashamed of passions that are natural and reasonable is generally proud of those that are shameful and silly.

~ *Lady Mary Wortley Montagu*

All of the men on my staff can type.

~ *Bella Abzug*

It is well within the order of things that man should listen when his mate sings; but the true male never yet walked who liked to listen when his mate talked.

~ *Anna Wickham*

The female of the genus homo is economically dependent on the male. He is her food supply.

~ *Charlotte P. Gilman*

The test of man is how well he is able to feel about what he thinks. The test of a woman is how well she is able to think about what she feels.

~ *Mary McDowell*

My husband thinks he's compromising if we have one cook instead of three.

~ *Ellen Barkin*

No, I don't understand my husband's theory of relativity, but I know my husband and I know he can be trusted.

~ *Elsa Einstein*

What, do you think feminism means you hate men?

~ *Cyndi Lauper*

A woman's dress should be like a barbed-wire fence: serving its purpose without obstructing the view.

~ *Sophia Loren*

I wanted to make it really special on Valentine's day, so I tied my boyfriend up. And for three solid hours I watched whatever I wanted on TV.

~ *Tracy Smith*

A lady is smarter than a gentleman, maybe, she can sew a fine seam, she can have a baby, she can use her intuition instead of her brain, but she can't fold a paper in a crowded train.

~ *Phyllis McGinley*

A wife should no more take her husband's name than he should hers. My name is my identity and must not be lost.

~ *Lucy Stone*

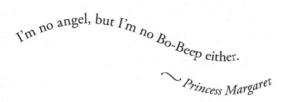

I'm no angel, but I'm no Bo-Beep either.

~ *Princess Margaret*

My husband said "show me your boobs" and I had to pull up my skirt . . . so it was time to get them done!

~ *Dolly Parton*

I don't need a man to
rectify my existence.
The most profound
relationship we'll ever have
is the one with ourselves.

~ *Shirley MacLaine*

My husband says
I feed him like he's
a God: every meal is
a burnt offering.

~ *Rhonda Hansome*

My husband does not like me to
give interviews because I say too
much. No talk, no trouble.

~ *Imelda Marcos*

If you want to sacrifice the admiration of many men for the criticism of one, go ahead, get married.

~ *Katharine Hepburn*

I was married for thirty years. Isn't that enough? I've had my share of dirty underwear on the floor.

~ *Martha Stewart*

Ducking for apples—change one letter and it's the story of my life.

~ *Dorothy Parker*

Men on Women

{ Love and Life with the Opposite Sex }

EDITED BY BARB KARG

ADAMS MEDIA
AVON, MASSACHUSETTS

Copyright © 2007, F+W Publications, Inc.

Published by
Adams Media, an F+W Publications Company
57 Littlefield Street
Avon, MA 02322. U.S.A.
www.adamsmedia.com

ISBN 10: 1-59337-732-0
ISBN 13: 978-1-59337-732-8

Printed in Canada.

J I H G F E D C B A

Library of Congress Cataloging-in-Publication Data
is available from the publisher.

This publication is designed to provide accurate and authoritative
information with regard to the subject matter covered. It is sold
with the understanding that the publisher is not engaged in
rendering legal, accounting, or other professional advice. If legal
advice or other expert assistance is required, the services of a
competent professional person should be sought.

—From a *Declaration of Principles* jointly adopted by a
Committee of the American Bar Association and
a Committee of Publishers and Associations

Many of the designations used by manufacturers and sellers to
distinguish their product are claimed as trademarks. Where those
designations appear in this book and Adams Media was aware of
a trademark claim, the designations have been printed with initial
capital letters.

This book is available at quantity discounts for bulk purchases.
For information, please call 1-800-289-0963.

FOR SISSY

*May your life be filled with love, peace, joy, and
comfort. And if all else fails—try chocolate.*

AND FOR RICK

My life, my love.

ACKNOWLEDGMENTS

Many fine individuals took part in the making of this book. As always, I'd like to thank Rick, Ma, Pop, Chris, Glen, Dad, Anne, Terry, Kathy, the Blonde Bombshell, Ellen, Jeans, all the Jims, Karla, and the Scribe Tribe. I adore you all.

I'd also like to extend a big thank you to the fine folks at Adams Media for all their hard work, including acquisitions editor extraordinaire Paula Munier, assistant editor Andrea Norville, associate production editor Casey Ebert, and senior book designer Colleen Cunningham. A shout goes out as well to Laura Daly, Brett Palana-Shanahan, Meredith O'Hayre, Rachel Engelson, and Sue Beale.

And lest I forget, I'd like to thank all the local espresso shops and the entire cast of *South Park* for keeping me awake and laughing throughout this process.

—*Barb Karg*

Introduction

EVER SINCE THE ARRIVAL of Eve, men have
found reason to alternately adore and admonish their better halves. Shakespeare marveled
at their frailty. Napoleon felt they were procreation machines. Freud could never crack the
feminine mystique. From Plato to present, the
male species remains forever vexed by creatures
of the fairer sex, and it's safe to say they probably
always will.

Fortunately for women, the term *suffrage* isn't
as viable a term as it used to be. A progression
of female history can be easily tracked by quotable males of the era, and while some opinions
remain narrow-minded and excessive, others
have taken baby steps toward a higher plane of
understanding.

No matter the male stance on a particular
physical or emotional subject, all observations
retain a certain element of humor and charm.
After all, without Eve, the Garden of Eden
would have been just another sports bar filled
with grouchy blokes pining for the affections of
a pretty woman.

"   "
. . .

Women are considered deep—
why? Because one can never
discover any bottom to them.
Women are not even shallow.

~ Friedrich Nietzsche

**A beautiful lady is an accident
of nature. A beautiful old
lady is a work of art.**

~ Louis Nizer

Women are an alien race
set down among us.

~ John Updike

**An extravagance is anything you buy
that is of no earthly use to your wife.**

~ Franklin Adams

I was married by a judge. I should have asked for a jury.

~ *Groucho Marx*

I'm glad I'm not bisexual;
I couldn't stand being rejected
by men as well as women.

~ *Bernard Manning*

Happiness is watching the TV at your girlfriend's house during a power failure.

~ *Bob Hope*

As long as a woman can look ten years younger than her own daughter, she is perfectly satisfied.

~ *Oscar Wilde*

When women kiss it
always reminds me of prize
fighters shaking hands.

~ *H. L. Mencken*

Wild horses couldn't drag a
secret out of most women.
However, women seldom have
lunch with wild horses.

~ *Ivern Boyett*

A woman's mind is
cleaner than a man's.
That's because she
changes it more often.

~ *Oliver Hereford*

To get over my divorce, I got
a prescription to live at the
Playboy Mansion for a while.

~ *James Caan*

My wife is the sort of woman who
gives necrophilia a bad name.

~ *Patrick Murray*

If there is reincarnation, I'd
like to come back as Warren
Beatty's fingertips.

~ *Woody Allen*

Thy wife is a constellation of virtues; she's the moon, and thou art the man in the moon.

~ *William Congreve*

An ideal wife is any woman who has an ideal husband.

~ *Booth Tarkington*

Alimony is like buying oats for a dead horse.

~ *Louis Saffan*

She looked as if she'd been poured into her clothes and had forgotten to say when.

~ *P. G. Wodehouse*

It requires nothing
less than a chivalric
feeling to sustain a
conversation with a lady.

~ *Henry David Thoreau*

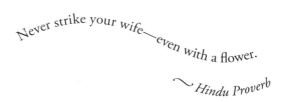

If there hadn't been women
we'd still be squatting in a cave
eating raw meat, because we
made civilization in order to
impress our girl friends. And
they tolerated it and let us go
ahead and play with our toys.

~ *Orson Welles*

To be born woman is to know—
although they do not speak
of it at school—women must
labor to be beautiful.

~ *William Butler Yeats*

The closest thing
to Roseanne Barr's
singing the national
anthem was my cat
being neutered.

~ *Johnny Carson*

Men who don't understand
women fall into two groups:
Bachelors and Husbands.

~ *Jacques Languirand*

To behold her is an immediate check to loose behavior; to love her is a liberal education.

〜 *Sir Richard Steele*

I have no hesitation in saying that although the American woman never leaves her domestic sphere and is in some respects very dependent within it, nowhere does she enjoy a higher station. And if anyone asks me what I think the chief cause of the extraordinary prosperity and growing power of this nation, I should answer that it is due to the superiority of their women.

〜 *Alexis De Tocqueville*

There are some women who should barely be spoken to; they should only be caressed.

〜 *Edgar Degas*

I have learned that only two things are necessary to keep one's wife happy. First, let her think she's having her own way. And second, let her have it.

⌒ *Lyndon B. Johnson*

There is one thing I would break up over and that is if she caught me with another woman. I wouldn't stand for that.

⌒ *Steve Martin*

A nice man is a man of nasty ideas.

⌒ *Jonathan Swift*

Where would man be today if it wasn't for women? In the Garden of Eden eating watermelon and taking it easy.

⌒ *C. Kennedy*

Being a woman is a
terribly difficult task since
it consists principally
in dealing with men.

~ *Joseph Conrad*

**A good wife always forgives her
husband when she's wrong.**

~ *Milton Berle*

A woman's guess is much more accurate than a man's certainty.

~ *Rudyard Kipling*

If you cannot inspire a woman
with love of you, fill her above
the brim with love of herself; all
that runs over will be yours.

~ *Charles Caleb Colton*

Women need a reason to have sex. Men just need a place.

~ *Billy Crystal*

When I was a young man I vowed never to marry until I found the ideal woman. Well, I found her but, alas, she was waiting for the ideal man.

~ *Robert Schuman*

I chased a girl for two years only to discover that her tastes were exactly like mine: We were both crazy about girls.

~ *Groucho Marx*

**No man should marry until
he has studied anatomy and
dissected at least one woman.**

~ *Honoré de Balzac*

If women are expected to do the same work as men, we must teach them the same things.

~ *Saul Bellow*

There's a difference between
beauty and charm. A beautiful
woman is one I notice. A charming
woman is one who notices me.

~ *John Erskine*

A husband is a guy who tells you when you've got on too much lipstick and helps you with your girdle when your hips stick.

~ *Ogden Nash*

Men are only as loyal as their options.

~ *Bill Maher*

There are no woman composers, never have been and possibly never will be.

~ *Sir Thomas Beecham*

The woman who is known only through a man is known wrong.

~ *Henry Brooks Adams*

When a man opens the car door for his wife, it's either a new car or a new wife.

~ *Prince Philip, Duke of Edinburgh*

Women like silent men.
They think they're listening.

~ *Marcel Archard*

Nobody can misunderstand a boy like his own mother. Mothers at present can bring children into the world, but this performance is apt to mark the end of their capacities. They can't even attend to the elementary animal requirements of their offspring. It is quite surprising how many children survive in spite of their mothers.

~ *Norman Douglas*

An ideal wife is one who remains faithful to you but tries to be just as charming as if she weren't.

~ *Sacha Guitry*

I don't think I'll get married again. I'll just find a woman I don't like and give her a house.

~ *Lewis Grizzard*

If men knew all that women think, they'd be twenty times more daring.

~ *Alphonse Karr*

I hate women because they always know where things are.

~ *Voltaire*

. . . it's a sort of bloom on a woman. If you have it you don't need to have anything else; and if you don't have it, it doesn't much matter what else you have.

⁓ *Sir James Matthew Barrie*

I haven't spoken to my wife in years. I didn't want to interrupt her.

⁓ *Rodney Dangerfield*

Men play the game; women know the score.

⁓ *Roger Woddis*

The Woman-Soul leadeth us upward and on!

⁓ *Johann Wolfgang von Goethe*

Observe this, that tho a woman swear, forswear, lie, dissemble, back-bite, be proud, vain, malicious, anything, if she secures the main chance, she's still virtuous; that's a maxim.

~ *George Farquhar*

Men are superior to women. For one thing, men can urinate from a speeding car.

~ *Will Durst*

That's the nature of women not to love when we love them, and to love when we love them not.

~ *Miguel de Cervantes*

Women who seek to
be equal with men
lack ambition.

~ *Timothy Leary*

A man falls in love through his
eyes, a woman through her ears.

~ *Thomas Carlyle*

**It is the woman who chooses the
man who will choose her.**

~ *Paul Geraldy*

Ne'er take a wife till thou
hast a house (and a
fire) to put her in.

~ *Benjamin Franklin*

Men don't know much about women.
We do know when they're happy.
We know when they're crying, and
we know when they're pissed off.
We just don't know in what order
these are gonna come at us.

~ *Evan Davis*

A woman drove me
to drink and I didn't
even have the decency
to thank her.

~ *W. C. Fields*

He knows little, who will tell
his wife all he knows.

~ *Thomas Fuller*

Women are most fascinating between the ages of thirty-five and forty, after they have won a few races and know how to pace themselves. Since few women ever pass forty, maximum fascination can continue indefinitely.

~ *Christian Dior*

She was not a women likely to settle for equality when sex gave her an advantage.

~ *Anthony Delano*

A new biography of Madonna came out last week, and apparently the biography lists all the men she's slept with. The book is apparently called the Manhattan Telephone Directory.

~ *Bill Maher*

Whatever else is unsure in this stinking dunghill of a world a mother's love is not.

~ *James Joyce*

It takes that *je ne sais quoi* which we call sophistication for a woman to be magnificent in a drawing-room when her faculties have departed but she herself has not yet gone home.

~ *James Thurber*

You know that look women get when they want sex? Me neither.

~ *Steve Martin*

It's my girl that advises. She has the head. But I never own to it before her. Discipline must be maintained.

~ *Charles Dickens*

If it were not somewhat fanciful to suppose that every human excellence is presented, as it were, in one kind of being, we might believe that the whole treasure of morality and order is enshrined in the female character.

~ *Karl Wilhelm Von Humboldt*

If a woman insists on being called Ms, ask her if it stands for miserable.

~ *Russell Bell*

The girl with a future avoids a man with a past.

~ *Evan Esar*

A lady is nothing very specific. One man's lady is another man's woman; sometimes, one man's lady is another man's wife. Definitions overlap but they almost never coincide.

~ *Russell Lynes*

A man should be taller, older, heavier, uglier and hoarser than his wife.

~ *Edgar Watson Howe*

The promises of maniacs, like those of women, are not safely relied upon.

~ *Joseph Heller*

Why should I limit myself to only one woman when I can have as many women as I want?

~ *George Gershwin*

No man knows more about women than I do, and I know nothing.

~ *Seymour Hicks*

When I have one foot in the grave, I will tell the whole truth about women. I shall tell it, jump into my coffin, pull the lid over me and say, "Do what you like now."

~ *Leo Tolstoy*

I buy women shoes and they use them to walk away from me.

~ *Mickey Rooney*

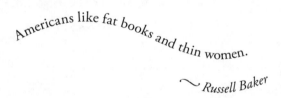

Americans like fat books and thin women.

~ *Russell Baker*

Here's to woman! Would that we could fold into her arms without falling into her hands.

~ *Ambrose Bierce*

Women's intuition is the result of millions of years of not thinking.

~ *Rupert Hughes*

When you see a woman who can go nowhere without a staff of admirers, it is not so much because they think she is beautiful, it is because she has told them they are handsome.

~ *Jean Giraudoux*

The superiority of one man's opinion over another's is never so great as when the opinion is about a woman.

~ *Henry James*

God gave us all a penis and a brain, but only enough blood to run one at a time.

~ *Robin Williams*

A Frenchwoman, when double-crossed, will kill her rival; the Italian woman would rather kill her deceitful lover; the Englishwoman simply breaks off relations; but they all will console themselves with another man.

~ *Charles Boyer*

One should never trust a woman who tells one her real age. A woman who would tell one that would tell one anything.

~ *Oscar Wilde*

She is not made to be
the admiration of all, but
the happiness of one.

~ *Edmund Burke*

A pessimist is a man who thinks
all women are bad. An optimist
is a man who hopes they are.

~ *Chauncey Depew*

Whether they give or refuse, it delights
women just the same to have been asked.

~ *Ovid*

The only way for a woman to
provide for herself decently is for
her to be good to some man that
can afford to be good to her.

~ *George Bernard Shaw*

Women of quality are so civil,
you can hardly distinguish
love from good breeding.

~ *William Wycherley*

Women are nothing but machines
for producing children.

~ *Napoleon Bonaparte*

If women didn't exist, all
the money in the world
would have no meaning.

~ *Aristotle Onassis*

What would men be without
women? Scarce, sir, mighty scarce.

~ *Mark Twain*

A woman is an occasional pleasure,
but a cigar is always a smoke.

~ *Groucho Marx*

I recently read that love
is entirely a matter of
chemistry. That must
be why my wife treats
me like toxic waste.

~ *David Bissonette*

It destroys one's nerves to
be amiable every day to
the same human being.

~ *Benjamin Disraeli*

Marriage is like putting your
hand into a bag of snakes in the
hope of pulling out an eel.

~ *Leonardo Da Vinci*

I chose my wife, as she did her wedding gown, for qualities that would wear well.

~ *Oliver Goldsmith*

A highbrow is a man who has found something more interesting than women.

~ *Edgar Wallace*

The great living experience for every man is his adventure into the woman. The man embraces in the woman all that is not himself, and from that one resultant, from that embrace, comes every new action.

~ *D. H. Lawrence*

I would go out with women my age, but there are no women my age.

~ *George Burns*

Men act and women appear.
Men look at women. Women watch
themselves being looked at.

~ *John Berger*

Such a wife as I want . . . must be
young, handsome I lay most stress
upon a good shape, sensible a little
learning will do, well-bred, chaste,
and tender. As to religion, a moderate
stock will satisfy me. She must
believe in God and hate a saint.

~ *Alexander Hamilton*

A diplomat is a man who
always remembers
a woman's birthday but
never remembers her age.

~ *Robert Frost*

The society of women is the
element of good manners.

~ *Johann Wolfgang von Goethe*

I feel like Zsa Zsa
Gabor's sixth husband.
I know what I'm supposed
to do, but I don't know
how to make it interesting.

~ *Milton Berle*

Man is a natural polygamist. He always has one woman leading him by the nose and another hanging on to his coattails.

~ *H. L. Mencken*

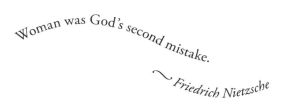

Woman was God's second mistake.

~ *Friedrich Nietzsche*

I don't think silicone makes a girl good or bad.

~ *James Caan*

No woman marries for money; they are all clever enough, before marrying a millionaire, to fall in love with him first.

~ *Cesare Pavese*

Mistress: Something
between a mister
and a mattress.

~ *Anonymous*

**I'm not against half
naked girls—not as often
as I'd like to be.**

~ *Benny Hill*

A man is already halfway in love with
any woman who listens to him.

~ *Brendan Francis*

**Girls are like butterflies . . . pretty
to look at, too hard to catch.**

~ *Unknown*

Women: If they're not turning down your proposals for marriage, they're accusing you of suspicious behavior in the women's lingerie changing room.

~ *Cliff Clavin*

Heav'n hath no rage like love to hatred turn'd, Nor Hell a fury, like a woman scorn'd.

~ *William Congreve*

Never let a beautiful woman pick your path for you when there is a man in her line of sight.

~ *Terry Goodkind*

What breadth, what beauty and power
of human nature and development
there must be in a woman to get
over all the palisades, all the fences,
within which she is held captive!

~ *Alexander Herzen*

For my part I distrust all
generalizations about women,
favorable and unfavorable,
masculine and feminine,
ancient and modern; all
alike, I should say, result from
paucity of experience.

~ *Bertrand Russell*

Sensible and responsible
women do not
want to vote.

~ *Grover Cleveland*

You should never say anything to a woman that even remotely suggests that you think she's pregnant unless you can see an actual baby emerging from her at that moment.

~ *Dave Barry*

The supply of good women far exceeds that of the men who deserve them.

~ *Robert Graves*

I'm the only man in the world with a marriage license made out to whom it may concern.

~ *Mickey Rooney*

Most women are not as young as they are painted.

~ Max Beerbohm

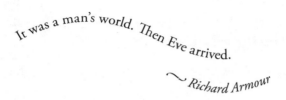

~ Richard Armour

Give a woman a job and she grows balls.

~ Jack Gelber

Variability is one of the virtues of a woman. It avoids the crude requirement of polygamy. So long as you have one good wife you are sure to have a spiritual harem.

~ G. K. Chesterton

I asked a Burmese why women, after centuries of following their men, now walk ahead. He said there were many unexploded land mines since the war.

~ *Robert Mueller*

Being a lady is an attitude.

~ *Chuck Woolery*

I would rather trust a woman's instinct than a man's reason.

~ *Stanley Baldwin*

They may talk of a comet, or a burning mountain, or some such bagatelle; but to me a modest woman, dressed out in all her finery, is the most tremendous object of the whole creation.

~ *Oliver Goldsmith*

Women are like cars: we all want a Ferrari, sometimes want a pickup truck, and end up with a station wagon.

~ *Tim Allen*

The simple lack of her is more to me than others' presence.

~ *Edward Thomas*

The age of a woman doesn't mean a thing. The best tunes are played on the oldest fiddles.

~ *Sigmund Z. Engel*

Marriage is a bribe to make the housekeeper think she's a householder.

~ *Thornton Wilder*

Women should have labels
on their foreheads saying,
"Government Health Warning:
women can seriously damage
your brains, genitals, current
account, confidence, razor
blades, and good standing
among your friends."

~ *Jeffrey Bernard*

By all means, marry. If
you get a good wife,
you'll become happy; if
you get a bad one, you'll
become a philosopher.

~ *Socrates*

They say marriages are made in Heaven. But so is thunder and lightning.

~ *Clint Eastwood*

There is no kind of harassment that a man may not inflict on a woman with impunity in civilized societies.

~ **Denis Diderot**

An ounce of mother is worth a pound of clergy.

~ *Spanish Proverb*

The true republic: men, their rights and nothing more; women, their rights and nothing less.

~ *Franklin P. Adams*

My mother-in-law broke up my marriage. My wife came home from work one day and found me in bed with her.

~ *Lenny Bruce*

Every woman is a rebel, and usually in wild revolt against herself.

~ *Oscar Wilde*

A good husband makes a good wife.

~ *John Florio*

As Miss America, my goal is to bring peace to the entire world and then get my own apartment.

~ *Jay Leno*

Only a male intellect clouded by the sexual drive could call the stunted, narrow-shouldered, broad-hipped and short-legged sex the fair sex.

~ *Arthur Schopenhauer*

Of all things upon earth that bleed and grow, a herb most bruised is woman.

~ *Euripides*

There are only three things to be done with a woman. You can love her, suffer for her, or turn her into literature.

~ *Lawrence Durrell*

If a woman has to choose between catching a fly ball and saving an infant's life, she will choose to save the infant's life without even considering if there are men on base.

~ *Dave Barry*

What are the three words guaranteed to humiliate men everywhere? "Hold my purse."

~ *Francois Morency*

I have always thought that every woman should marry, and no man.

~ *Benjamin Disraeli*

Like most men, I am consumed with desire whenever a lesbian gets within twenty feet.

~ *Taki*

You don't appreciate a lot of stuff in school until you get older. Little things like being spanked every day by a middle-aged woman: Stuff you pay good money for in later life.

~ *Emo Philips*

Men marry to make an end; women to make a beginning.

~ *Alexis Dupuy*

A lady of forty-seven who had been married twenty-seven years and has six children knows what love really is and once described it for me like this: "Love is what you've been through with somebody."

~ *James Thurber*

It is an extra dividend when you like the girl you've fallen in love with.

~ *Clark Gable*

Next to coming to a good understanding with a new mistress, I love a quarrel with an old one.

~ *Sir George Etherege*

These impossible women!
How they do get around
us! The poet was right:
Can't live with them,
or without them.

~ *Aristophanes*

Women hate everything which
strips off the tinsel of sentiment,
and they are right, or it would
rob them of their weapons.

~ *Lord Byron*

A study in the *Washington Post*
says that women have better
verbal skills than men.
I just want to say to the
authors of that study: Duh.

~ *Conan O'Brien*

We have dreamt of every woman there is, and dreamt too of the miracle that would bring us the pleasure of being a woman, for women have all the qualities— courage, passion, the capacity to love, cunning—whereas all our imagination can do is naively pile up the illusion of courage.

~ *Jean Baudrillard*

I expect that Woman will be the last thing civilized by Man.

~ *George Meredith*

Direct thought is not an attribute of femininity. In this, women are now centuries behind man.

~ *Thomas Edison*

Many a man owes
his success to his first
wife, and his second
wife to his success.

~ *Jim Backus*

Women are like elephants.
Everyone likes to look
at them but no-one likes
to have to keep one.

~ *W. C. Fields*

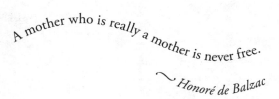

A mother who is really a mother is never free.

~ *Honoré de Balzac*

A man's only as old as
the woman he feels.

~ *Groucho Marx*

Woman's destiny is to be wanton, like the bitch, the she-wolf; she must belong to all who claim her.

~ *Marquis de Sade*

You've got many refinements. I don't think you need to worry about your failure at long division. I mean, after all, you got through short division, and short division is all that a lady ought to be called on to cope with.

~ *Tennessee Williams*

Frailty, thy name is woman!

~ *William Shakespeare*

In my house I'm the boss, my wife is just the decision maker.

~ *Woody Allen*

When the candles are out all women are fair.

~ *Plutarch*

When a man talks dirty to a woman, it's sexual harassment. When a woman talks dirty to a man, it's $3.95 a minute.

~ *Author Unknown*

Lovely female shapes are terrible complicators of the difficulties and dangers of this earthly life, especially for their owners.

~ *George du Maurier*

The soundtrack to *Indecent Exposure* is a romantic mix of music that I know most women love to hear, so I never keep it far from me when women are nearby.

~ *Fabio*

I have an idea that the phrase "weaker sex" was coined by some woman to disarm some man she was preparing to overwhelm.

~ *Ogden Nash*

Be to her virtues very kind, Be to her faults a little blind.

~ *Matthew Prior*

I'd rather have
two girls at
seventeen than
one at thirty-four.

~ *Fred Allen*

If President Nixon's secretary,
Rosemary Woods, had been
Moses' secretary, there would
only be eight commandments.

~ *Art Buchwald*

It is only rarely that one
can see in a little boy
the promise of a man,
but one can almost
always see in a little girl
the threat of a woman.

~ *Alexandre Dumas*

Well-married, a man is winged: ill-matched, he is shackled.

~ *Henry Ward Beecher*

My wife has a slight impediment in her speech. Every now and then she stops to breathe.

~ *Jimmy Durante*

You see, dear, it is not true that woman was made from man's rib; she was really made from his funny bone.

~ *Sir James Matthew Barrie*

Of all the rights of women, the greatest is to be a mother.

~ *Lin Yutang*

I almost got a girl pregnant
in high school. It's costing me
a fortune to keep the rabbit
on a life-support system.

~ Will Shriner

The way to fight a woman is with
your hat. Grab it and run.

~ John Barrymore

I have good-looking
kids. Thank goodness
my wife cheats on me.

~ Rodney Dangerfield

Patience makes a woman
beautiful in middle age.

~ Elliot Paul

While farmers generally allow one rooster for ten hens, ten men are scarcely sufficient to service one woman.

~ *Giovanni Boccaccio*

If a woman hasn't got a tiny streak of harlot in her, she's a dry stick as a rule.

~ *D. H. Lawrence*

Any husband who says "My wife and I are completely equal partners," is talking about either a law firm or a hand of bridge.

~ *Bill Cosby*

Nature intended women to be our slaves. They are our property.

~ *Napoleon Bonaparte*

There is only one real tragedy in a woman's life. The fact that her past is always her lover, and her future invariably her husband.

~ *Oscar Wilde*

Men have a much better time of it than women: for one thing they marry later, for another thing they die earlier.

~ *H. L. Mencken*

There are many examples of women that have excelled in learning, and even in war, but this is no reason we should bring em all up to Latin and Greek or else military discipline, instead of needle-work and housewifery.

~ *Bernard Mandeville*

I told my wife that a husband is like a fine wine; he gets better with age. The next day, she locked me in the cellar.

~ *Anonymous*

When a woman becomes a scholar there is usually something wrong with her sexual organs.

~ *Friedrich Nietzsche*

Never feel remorse for what you have thought about your wife; she has thought much worse things about you.

~ *Jean Rostand*

A woman knows the face of the man she loves as a sailor knows the open sea.

~ *Honoré de Balzac*

I always cry at weddings, especially my own.

~ *Humphrey Bogart*

There's two theories to arguing with a woman. Neither one works.

~ *Will Rogers*

The essence of life is
the smile of round
female bottoms,
under the shadow of
cosmic boredom.

~ *Guy de Maupassant*

Do you know what it means to come
home at night to a woman who'll give
you a little love, a little affection, a
little tenderness? It means you're in the
wrong house, that's what it means.

~ *George Burns*

Every woman is wrong
until she cries, and then
she is right, instantly.

~ *Thomas C. Haliburton*

A woman can laugh and cry in three seconds and it's not weird. But if a man does it, it's very disturbing. The way I'd describe it is like this: I have been allowed inside the house of womanhood, but I feel that they wouldn't let me in any of the interesting rooms.

~ Rob Schneider

Even if man could understand women he still wouldn't believe it.

~ AW Brown

Women upset everything.
When you let them into your
life, you find that the woman
is driving at one thing and
you're driving at another.

~ *George Bernard Shaw*

A man must marry only
a very pretty woman
in case he should ever
want some other man to
take her off his hands.

~ *Sacha Guitry*

The only time my wife and
I had a simultaneous orgasm
was when the judge signed
the divorce papers.

~ *Woody Allen*

Slavery it is that makes slavery; freedom, freedom. The slavery of women happened when the men were slaves of kings.

~ *Ralph Waldo Emerson*

Bride: A woman with a fine prospect of happiness behind her.

~ *Ambrose Bierce*

All men make mistakes, but married men find out about them sooner.

~ *Red Skelton*

Don't tell a woman she's pretty; tell her there's no other woman like her, and all roads will open to you.

~ *Jules Renard*

How marriage ruins a man! It is as demoralizing as cigarettes, and far more expensive.

~ *Oscar Wilde*

Sure God created man before woman. But then you always make a rough draft before the final masterpiece.

~ *Unknown*

I could sooner reconcile all Europe than two women.

~ *Louis XIV*

Give me golf clubs, fresh
air and a beautiful partner,
and you can keep the
clubs and the fresh air.

~ *Jack Benny*

A woman can say more in a sigh
than a man can say in a sermon.

~ *Arnold Haultain*

And behind every man who's a
failure there's a woman, too!

~ *John Ruge*

Every girl should use
what Mother Nature
gave her before Father
Time takes it away.

~ *Laurence J. Peter*

Blondes make the best victims. They're like virgin snow that shows up the bloody footprints.

~ *Alfred Hitchcock*

Next to the wound, what women make best is the bandage.

~ *Jules Barbey d'Aurevilly*

There's something luxurious about having a girl light your cigarette. In fact, I got married once on account of that.

~ *Harold Robbins*

The woman who tells her age is either too young to have anything to lose or too old to have anything to gain.

~ *Chinese Proverb*

On the one hand, we'll never experience childbirth. On the other hand, we can open all our own jars.

~ *Bruce Willis*

If a girl looks swell when she meets you, who gives a damn if she's late? Nobody.

~ *J. D. Salinger*

It is the woman who chooses the man who will choose her.

~ *Paul Géraldy*

I've reached the age where competence is a turn-on.

~ *Billy Joel*

All the men in my family were bearded, and most of the women.

~ *W. C. Fields*

Women do not find it difficult nowadays to behave like men, but they often find it extremely difficult to behave like gentlemen.

~ *Compton Mackenzie*

Now that women are jockeys, baseball umpires, atomic scientists, and business executives, maybe someday they can master parallel parking.

~ *Bill Vaughn*

Women have a passion for mathematics. They divide their age in half, double the price of their clothes, and always add at least five years to the age of their best friend.

~ *Marcel Achard*

Earth's noblest thing, a Woman perfected.

~ *James Russell Lowell*

Don't you realize that as long as you have to sit down to pee, you'll never be a dominant force in the world? You'll never be a convincing technocrat or middle manager. Because people will know. She's in there sitting down.

~ *Don DeLillo*

Most women have no characters at all.

~ *Alexander Pope*

Woman—for example, look at her case!
She turns tantalizing inviting glances
on you. You seize her. No sooner does
she feel herself in your grasp than
she closes her eyes. It is a sign of her
mission, the sign by which she says to
man: Blind yourself, for I am blind.

~ *Luigi Pirandello*

Much can be inferred about
a man from his mistress:
in her one beholds his
weaknesses and his dreams.

~ *Georg C. Lichtenberg*

If you go to see
the woman, do not
forget the whip.

~ *Friedrich Nietzsche*

Every man who is high up loves to think that he has done it all himself; and the wife smiles, and lets it go at that.

~ *Sir James Matthew Barrie*

I know you've been married to the same woman for 69 years. That is marvelous. It must be very inexpensive.

~ *Johnny Carson*

Marriage is the alliance of two people, one of whom never remembers birthdays and the other never forgets them.

~ *Ogden Nash*

If women ran the world
we wouldn't have wars,
just intense negotiations
every twenty-eight days.

~ *Robin Williams*

No one knows like a woman
how to say things, which are
at once gentle and deep.

~ *Victor Hugo*

Men at most differ as Heaven
and Earth, but women, worst and
best, as Heaven and Hell.

~ *Alfred Lord Tennyson*

Beauty Parlor: A place where
women curl up and dye.

~ *Aiken Drum*

A woman's whole life is a history of the affections.

~ *Washington Irving*

Once a woman has given you her heart, you can never get rid of the rest of her.

~ *John Vanbrugh*

Those hot pants of hers were so damned tight, I could hardly breathe.

~ *Benny Hill*

The little rift between the sexes is astonishingly widened by simply teaching one set of catchwords to the girls and another to the boys.

~ *Robert Louis Stevenson*

Nature has given women so much power that the law has very wisely given them little.

~ *Samuel Johnson*

Many a man in love with a dimple makes a mistake of marrying the whole girl.

~ *Stephen Leacock*

Imagine what will happen to this nation if large numbers of American women start using the Wonderbra. It will be catastrophic. The male half of the population will be nothing but mindless drooling Zombies of Lust. Granted, this is also true now, but it will be even worse.

~ *Dave Barry*

'Tis strange what a man may do, and a woman yet think him an angel.

~ *William Makepeace Thackeray*

Men want a woman whom they can turn on and off like a light switch.

~ *Ian Fleming*

Women wear the breeches.

~ *Robert Burton*

Strange to say what delight we married people have to see these poor fools decoyed into our condition.

~ *Samuel Pepys*

Behind every successful man is a woman, behind her is his wife.

~ *Groucho Marx*

Marriage is about the most expensive way for the average man to get laundry done.

~ *Burt Reynolds*

Women who can, do. Those who can't become feminists.

~ *Bobby Riggs*

An undutiful Daughter will prove an unmanageable Wife.

~ *Benjamin Franklin*

As usual, there is a great woman behind every idiot.

~ *John Lennon*

If she seem not chaste to me,
What care I how chaste she be?

~ *Sir Walter Raleigh*

My wife has a whim of iron.

~ *Oliver Herford*

You don't know a women till
you've met her in court.

~ *Norman Mailer*

My wife is a sex object. Every
time I ask for sex, she objects.

~ *Les Dawson*

To find out a girl's faults,
praise her to her girl friends.

~ *Benjamin Franklin*

Don't have sex, man. It leads to
kissing and pretty soon you have
to start talking to them.

~ *Steve Martin*

What Women Want: To
be loved, to be listened
to, to be desired, to be
respected, to be needed,
to be trusted, and
sometimes, just to be held.
What Men Want: Tickets
for the World Series.

~ *Dave Barry*

Few misfortunes can befall a boy which
bring worse consequences than to
have a really affectionate mother.

~ *W. Somerset Maugham*

When women love us,
they forgive us everything,
even our crimes; when they
do not love us, they give
us credit for nothing,
not even our virtues.

~ *Honoré de Balzac*

All women are born
evil. Some just realize
their potential later
in life than others.

~ *Chad A. Gamble*

I love women. They're the best thing ever created. If they want to be like men and come down to our level, that's fine.

~ *Mel Gibson*

A man is as good as he has to be,
and a woman is as bad as she dares.

~ *Elbert Hubbard*

I was the best man at the wedding. If I'm the best man, why is she marrying him?

~ *Jerry Seinfeld*

A man is called a good fellow
for doing things which, if
done by a woman, would land
her in a lunatic asylum.

～ H. L. Mencken

Nobody will ever win the battle
of the sexes. There's too much
fraternizing with the enemy.

～ Henry Kissinger

Honolulu, it's got everything.
Sand for the children,
sun for the wife,
sharks for the wife's mother.

～ Ken Dodd

Not only is women's work never done,
the definition keeps changing.

~ *Bill Copeland*

No man is as anti-feminist as a really feminine woman.

~ *Frank O'Connor*

Women speak two languages—one of which is verbal.

~ *William Shakespeare*

Women now have choices.
They can be married, not married,
have a job, not have a job, be married
with children, unmarried with
children. Men have the same choice
we've always had: work or prison.

~ *Tim Allen*

There are three classes into which all the women past seventy that ever I knew were to be divided:
1. That dear old soul;
2. That old woman;
3. That old witch.

~ *Marcus Aurelius*

> It is a woman's business to get married as soon as possible, and a man's to keep unmarried as long as he can.
>
> ~ *George Bernard Shaw*

A good and true woman is said to resemble a Cremona fiddle—age but increases its worth and sweetens its tone.

~ *Oliver Wendell Holmes, Sr.*

My wife dresses to kill.
She cooks the same way.

~ *Henny Youngman*

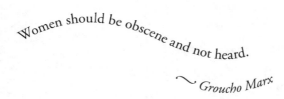

Women should be obscene and not heard.

~ *Groucho Marx*

A good cigar is as great a comfort to
a man as a good cry is to a woman.

~ *Edward G. Bulwer-Lytton*

Next to God we are
indebted to women, first
for life itself, and then for
making it worth having.

~ *Christian Nestell Bovee*

A woman watches her body uneasily, as though it were an unreliable ally in the battle for love.

~ *Leonard Cohen*

I am very fond of the company of ladies.
I like their beauty,
I like their delicacy,
I like their vivacity, and
I like their silence.

~ *Samuel Johnson*

Her stature tall—I hate a dumpy woman.

~ *Lord Byron*

I am not a cat man, but a dog man,
and all felines can tell this at a
glance—a sharp, vindictive glance.

~ *James Thurber*

Husbands never become good; they merely become proficient.

~ *H. L. Mencken*

Men are from Mars,
Women are from Venus.

~ *John Gray*

We're more effective than birth control pills.

~ *Johnny Carson*

A woman seldom asks
advice before she
has bought her
wedding clothes.

⌒ *Joseph Addison*

Marriage changes passion.
. . . Suddenly you're in
bed with a relative.

⌒ *Author Unknown*

Eighty percent of married
men cheat in America. The
rest cheat in Europe.

⌒ *Jackie Mason*

What men desire is a virgin
who is a whore.

⌒ *Edward Dahlbert*

A woman who gives any advantage to a man may expect a lover—but will sooner or later find a tyrant.

~ *Lord Byron*

My advice to the women's clubs of America is to raise more hell and fewer dahlias.

~ *William Allen White*

The test of civilization is the estimate of woman. Among savages she is a slave. In the dark ages of Christianity she is a toy and a sentimental goddess. With increasing moral light, and greater liberty, and more universal justice, she begins to develop as an equal human being.

~ *George William Curtis*

Men want the same thing from their underwear that they want from women: a little bit of support, and a little bit of freedom.

∼ *Jerry Seinfeld*

Choose a wife rather by your ear than your eye.

∼ *Thomas Fuller*

No one in the world needs
a mink coat but a mink.

∼ *Author Unknown*

A woman who cannot be
ugly is not beautiful.

∼ *Karl Kraus*

Some people ask the secret of our long marriage. We take time to go to a restaurant two times a week. A little candlelight, dinner, soft music and dancing. She goes Tuesdays, I go Fridays.

⁓ Henny Youngman

If you are ever in doubt as to whether to kiss a pretty girl, always give her the benefit of the doubt.

⁓ Thomas Carlyle

God help the man who won't marry until he finds a perfect woman, and God help him still more if he finds her.

⁓ Benjamin Tillett

There are a number
of mechanical devices that
increase sexual arousal,
particularly in women.
Chief amongst these is
the Mercedes-Benz
380L convertible.

~ *P. J. O'Rourke*

What ought to be
done to the man who
invented the celebrating
of anniversaries? Mere
killing would be too light.

~ *Mark Twain*

If the wife sins, the
husband is not innocent.

~ *Italian Proverb*

Women deserve to have more than twelve years between the ages of twenty-eight and forty.

~ *James Thurber*

Every time a woman leaves off something she looks better, but every time a man leaves off something he looks worse.

~ *Will Rogers*

I know many married men, I even know a few happily married men, but I don't know one who wouldn't fall down the first open coal hole running after the first pretty girl who gave him a wink.

~ *George Jean Nathan*

In every mess I find a friend,
In every port a wife.

~ *Charles Dibdin*

It is hard, if not impossible, to snub
a beautiful woman—they remain
beautiful and the snub recoils.

~ *Winston Churchill*

It's not a good idea to put
your wife into a novel; not
your latest wife anyway.

~ *Norman Mailer*

A woman should be an illusion.

~ *Ian Fleming*

You can calculate
Zsa Zsa Gabor's age by
the rings on her fingers.

~ *Bob Hope*

Nothing can be more absurd
than the practice that prevails
in our country of men and
women not following the same
pursuits with all their strengths
and with one mind, for thus,
the state instead of being
whole is reduced to half.

~ *Plato*

Men get laid, but
women get screwed.

~ *Quentin Crisp*

Women cannot complain
about men anymore
until they start getting
better taste in them.

~ *Bill Maher*

Women have a much better time
than men in this world. There are far
more things forbidden to them.

~ *Oscar Wilde*

The Russians love
Brooke Shields because
her eyebrows remind them
of Leonid Brezhnev.

~ *Robin Williams*

But to see her was to love her,
Love but her, and love forever.

~ *Robert Burns*

When a man steals your wife
there is no better revenge
than to let him keep her.

~ *Sacha Guitry*

I've had bad luck with
both my wives. The first
one left me and the
second one didn't.

~ *Patrick Murray*

Women: Can't live with them,
can't bury them in the back yard
without the neighbours seeing.

~ *Sean Williamson*

Women add zest to the unlicensed hours.

~ *Allen Thomas*

Despite my thirty years of research into the feminine soul, I have not yet been able to answer the great question that has never been answered: What does a woman want?

~ *Sigmund Freud*

Last week I stated that this woman was the ugliest woman I had ever seen. I have since been visited by her sister and now wish to withdraw that statement.

~ *Mark Twain*

I wouldn't be caught dead marrying a woman old enough to be my wife.

~ *Tony Curtis*

A woman's place is in the wrong.

~ *James Thurber*

Last time I tried to make love to my wife nothing was happening, so I said to her, "What's the matter, you can't think of anybody either?"

~ *Rodney Dangerfield*

The female of the species is more deadly than the male.

~ *Rudyard Kipling*

With women you don't
have to talk your head off.
You just say a word and let
them fill in from there.

~ *Satchel Paige*

Sex between a man and a
woman can be wonderful,
provided you can get
between the right man
and the right woman.

~ *Woody Allen*

A woman will buy anything
she thinks the store is
losing money on.

~ *Kin Hubbard*

To understand one woman is
not necessarily to understand
any other woman.

~ *John Stuart Mill*

I like clean ladies and nice ladies.

~ *Lawrence Welk*

**Epperson's law: When a man says it's
a silly, childish game, it's probably
something his wife can beat him at.**

~ *Don Epperson*

I kissed my first girl and
smoked my first cigarette
on the same day. I haven't
had time for tobacco since.

~ *Arturo Toscanini*

I wonder why it is, that young men are always cautioned against bad girls. Anyone can handle a bad girl. It's the good girls men should be warned against.

~ *David Niven*

Do you seriously expect me to be the first Prince of Wales in history not to have a mistress?

~ *Prince Charles*

Marriage: A master, a mistress and two slaves, making in all, two.

~ *Ambrose Bierce*

He who marries a widow will often have a dead man's head thrown in his dish.

~ *Spanish Proverb*

Ah, yes, divorce . . . from
the Latin word meaning
to rip out a man's genitals
through his wallet.

~ *Robin Williams*

I never expected to see the day
when girls would get sunburned
in the places they do today.

~ *Will Rogers*

In Hollywood, a starlet
is the name for any
woman under thirty
who is not actively
employed in a brothel.

~ *Ben Hecht*

Here's to our wives
and sweethearts—
may they never meet.

~ *John Bunny*

She was what we used to
call a suicide blonde—
dyed by her own hand.

~ *Saul Bellow*

Have you heard of the new
divorced Barbie doll? She comes
with all of Ken's stuff.

~ *Anonymous*

Men naturally resent it when
women take greater liberties in
dress than men are allowed.

~ *Michael Korda*

You know, men and women are a lot alike in certain situations. Like when they're both on fire—they're exactly alike.

~ *Dave Attell*

To succeed with the opposite sex, tell her you're impotent. She can't wait to disprove it.

~ *Cary Grant*

There are three intolerable things in life—cold coffee, lukewarm champagne, and overexcited women.

~ *Orson Welles*

Blondes have the hottest kisses. Redheads are fair-to-middling torrid, and brunettes are the frigidest of all. It's something to do with hormones, no doubt.

∼ *Ronald Reagan*

The Catholic men are more upset about women not being able to be priests than are Catholic women.

∼ *Andrew Greeley*

High heels were invented by a woman who had been kissed on the forehead.

∼ *Christopher Morley*

With women, I've got a long bamboo pole with a leather loop on the end of it. I slip the loop around their necks so they can't get away or come too close. Like catching snakes.

~ *Marlon Brando*

The penalty for getting the woman you want is that you must keep her.

~ *Lionel Strachey*

When you get married you forget about kissing other women.

~ *Pat Boone*

Any man who can drive safely while
kissing a pretty girl is simply not giving
the kiss the attention it deserves.

~ *Albert Einstein*

I like a woman with a
head on her shoulders.
I hate necks.

~ *Steve Martin*

Women and people of
low birth are very hard to
deal with. If you are friendly
with them, they get out of
hand, and if you keep your
distance, they resent it.

~ *Confucius*

I will not say that
women have no
character; rather,
they have a new
one every day.

~ *Heinrich Heine*

How much fame, money and
power does a woman have to
achieve on her own before you
can punch her in the face?

~ *P. J. O'Rourke*

The silliest woman can manage a
clever man; but it needs a clever
woman to manage a fool.

~ *Rudyard Kipling*

Before marriage a man
yearns for a woman.
Afterward the "y" is silent.

~ *W. A. Clarke*

The most romantic thing
a woman ever said to me
in bed was, "Are you sure
you're not a cop?"

~ *Larry Brown*

A man admires a woman
not for what she says, but
for what she listens to.

~ *George Jean Nathan*

The big difference between sex for money and sex for free is that sex for money usually costs a lot less.

~ *Brendan Behan*

Men are clinging to football on a level we aren't even aware of. For centuries, we ruled everything, and now, in the last ten minutes, there are all these incursions by women. It's our Alamo.

~ *Tony Kornheiser*

There's only one way to have a happy marriage and as soon as I learn what it is I'll get married again.

~ *Clint Eastwood*

The body of a young woman is God's
greatest achievement . . . Of course,
He could have built it to last longer
but you can't have everything.

〜 *Neil Simon*

Rich widows: The only
secondhand goods that
sell at first-class prices.

〜 *Benjamin Franklin*

Even the wisest men make fools
of themselves about women,
and even the most foolish
women are wise about men.

〜 *Theodore Reik*

Only men who are not interested in women are interested in women's clothes. Men who like women never notice what they wear.

~ Anatole France

**I have such poor vision
I can date anybody.**

~ Garry Shandling

Women do not win formula one races, because they simply are not strong enough to resist the G-forces. In the boardroom, it is different. I believe women are better able to marshal their thoughts than men, and because they are less egotistical, they make fewer assumptions.

~ Henry Ford

It's relaxing to go out with my ex-wife because she already knows I'm an idiot.

⌒ *Warren Thomas*

I like young girls.
Their stories are shorter.

⌒ *Tom McGuane*

No woman is worth the loss of a night's sleep.

⌒ *Sir Thomas Beecham*

No matter how happily a woman may be married, it always pleases her to discover that there is a nice man who wishes that she were not.

~ *H. L. Mencken*

In life, as in art, the beautiful moves in curves.

~ *Edward G. Bulwer-Lytton*

Women and cats will do as they please, and men and dogs should relax and get used to the idea.

~ *Robert A. Heinlein*

The rule in the women's colleges was that after seven P.M. all men were beasts. Up until seven P.M. they were all angels, and the girls simply had to learn to live with that routine and practice love in the afternoon.

⁓ *Harry G. Johnson*

The secret of a happy marriage remains a secret.

⁓ *Henny Youngman*

Then she rode forth,
clothed on with chastity:
The deep air listen'd
round her as she rode,
And all the low wind hardly
breathed for fear.

⁓ *Alfred Lord Tennyson*

Appendix: Resources for *Men on Women*

http://creativewit.com

http://cutechoice.com

http://en.proverbia.net

http://en.thinkexist.com

http://en.wikiquote.org

http://funny2.com

http://heather.creative-flow.net

http://home.att.net

http://home.neo.rr.com

http://jarday.com

http://koti.mbnet.fi/neptunia

http://likemom.com

http://littlecalamity.tripod.com

http://nonstopenglish.com

http://quotesandjokes.com

http://quotes.liberty-tree.ca

http://zaadz.com

www.1-famous-quotes.com/quotes

www.19.5degs.com

www.aardvarkarchie.com

www.allgreatquotes.com

www.allmyquotes.com

www.allthingswilliam.com

www.amazon.com

www.amusingquotes.com

www.animalliberationfront.com

www.anvari.org

www.aphids.com

www.bartleby.com

www.basicquotations.com

www.bellaonline.com

www.biggeworld.com

www.birthdaycelebrations.net

www.born-today.com

www.borntomotivate.com

www.brainyquote.com

www.comedy-zone.net

www.compleatsteve.com

www.coolquotescollection.com

www.corsinet.com/
braincandy/ins-fwm.html

www.creativequotations.com

www.crystalclouds.co.uk

www.dailycelebrations.com

www.deepbox.com

www.divorcehq.com

www.dribbleglass.com

www.famous-quotations.com

www.famous-quotes-
and-quotations.com

www.famous-quotes.com

www.funnybone.com

www.funnyjunk.com

www.geog.ucsb.edu

www.giga-usa.com

www.goodquotes.com

www.google.com

www.greatest-quotations.com

www.great-quotes.com

www.homemakingcottage.com

www.humorsphere.com

www.indianngos.com

www.inspirationalwoman.com

www.jokes-quotes.com

www.lifeisajoke.com

www.lovelandia.com

www.memorablequotations.com

www.mens.net

www.model-a-ford-gifts.com

www.mothers.net

www.netapt.com

www.nomarriage.com

www.oneliners-and-proverbs.com

www.poemhunter.com

www.quotationlibrary.com

www.quotationspage.com

www.quotedb.com

www.quotegarden.com

www.quoteland.com

www.quotemountain.com

www.quotesandsayings.com

www.quotes-zone.com

www.revisedevilsdictionary.com

www.saidwhat.co.uk

www.sbrowning.com

www.thatsrich.com/celeb.htm

www.theabsolute.net

www.thebestman.com

www.theholidayspot.com

www.thehumorarchives.com

www.theotherpages.org

www.tomstrong.org

www.wasted-education.com

www.weeks-g.dircon.co.uk

www.whimsy.org.uk

www.womens.net

www.workinghumor.com

www.worldofquotes.com

1,911 Best things anybody ever said, Robert Byrne, a Fawcett Columbine Book published by Ballantine Books, 1988.

Appendix: Resources for *Women on Men*

http://bowering.org
http://en.thinkexist.com
http://en.proverbia.net
http://heather.creative-flow.net
http://home.att.net
http://homepage.eircom.net
http://sfgate.com
http://techrepublic.com.com
http://womenshistory.about.com
http://zaadz.com
www.1-love-quotes.com
www.1-famous-quotes.com
www.aardvarkarchie.com
www.absolutely.com
www.allmovieportal.net
www.americanpoems.com
www.amusingquotes.com
www.anecdotage.com
www.angelfire.com
www.aphids.com
www.bartleby.com
www.batchmates.com
www.blondes.net
www.bookreporter.com
www.borntomotivate.com
www.brainyquotes.com
www.brownielocks.com

www.c-boom.com
www.cedarnet.org
www.cnn.com
www.coolquotes.com
www.comedy-zone.net
www.coolfunnyjokes.com
www.creativequotations.com
www.cs.virginia.
edu/~robins/quotes.html
www.divasthesite.com
www.empirezine.com
www.excite.com
www.famouscreativewomen.com
www.feminist.com
www.geocities.com
www.giga-usa.com
www.google.com
www.handbag.com
www.ihatemen.com
www.jokes2go.com
www.lifeisajoke.com
www.limarriages.com
www.lovelandia.com
www.lyricz.com
www.manhaters.com
www.margaretthatcher.com
www.mcwilliams.com

www.memorablequotations.com
www.mens.net
www.pinkmonkey.com
www.poemhunter.com
www.practicallyfamous.com
www.premierespeakers.com
www.quotationreference.com
www.quotationsbook.com
www.quotationspage.com
www.quotecha.com
www.quotedb.com
www.quotegarden.com
www.quotemountain.com
www.quotesforall.com
www.quotesonline.com
www.quoteworld.org
www.saidwhat.co.uk
www.seehomes.com
www.songlyrics.com
www.spicyquotes.com
www.theotherpages.org
www.tpub.com
www.unmarried.org
www.wendy.com
www.wikiquote.com
www.wisdomquotes.com
www.womenshistory.about.com
www.worldofquotes.com
www.yahoo.com
www.yourquotations.net

21st Century Dictionary of Quotations, Princeton Language Institute, 1993

The Columbia World of Quotations, Columbia University Press, 1996

On Being Blonde, Paula Munier, Fair Winds Press, 2004